POEMS FOR THE
GAME OF SILENCE

POEMS FOR THE GAME OF SILENCE

1960–1970

JEROME ROTHENBERG

A NEW DIRECTIONS BOOK

The poems from *White Sun Black Sun* & all of *Sightings I-IX* were origi-
nally published by Jerome Rothenberg's Hawk's Well Press. The author
wishes to extend thanks to the publishers of the following books from which
most of the other works in the present book have been gathered: *The Seven
Hells of the Jigoku Zoshi* (George Economou & Robert Kelly for Trobar
Books), *The Gorky Poems* (Sergio Mondragon & Margaret Randall for
El Corno Emplumado), *Ritual: A Book of Primitive Rites & Events* (Dick
Higgins for Something Else Press), *Between* (Stuart & Deirdre Montgomery
for Fulcrum Press), *The Flight of Quetzalcoatl* (Bill Butler for Unicorn-
Brighton), *Conversations & Poems 1964–1967* (John Martin for Black Spar-
row Press), *Technicians of the Sacred* (Doubleday & Co.), *Sightings & Red
Easy A Color* (Ian Tyson for Circle Books), *The 17 Horse-Songs of Frank
Mitchell* (Tyson too for Tetrad Books), & *Poland/1931* (Alan Brilliant
for Unicorn Press). Acknowledgments & thanks are also due the editors of
the following anthologies & magazines, where many of these works have
appeared: *A Controversy of Poets* (ed. Kelly & Leary), *The East Side
Scene* (ed. DeLoach), *The New Modern Poetry* (ed. Rosenthal), *Nota-
tions* (ed. Cage), *Inside Outer Space* (ed. Vas Dias), *Manifestos* (ed. Hig-
gins), *The New Open Poetry* (ed. Quasha, et al.), *A Caterpillar Anthology*
(ed. Eshleman), & *Alcheringa, Alpha Sort, Ant's Forefoot, Between Worlds,
Caterpillar, Chelsea, Damascus Road, 11th Finger, The Fifties, Friendly
Local Press, I • kon, Kansas Write-In, Kulchur, The Nation, New Measure,
Nomad, Plumed Horn, Poems from the Floating World, Poetry, Pogamog-
gan, Poor • Old • Tired • Horse, San Francisco Review, some/thing, Stony
Brook, Trobar, WIN,* & *0 to 9.* All materials in *Sightings: Kunapipi* are
from aboriginal songs translated in R. M. Berndt's *Kunapipi: A Study of
an Australian Aboriginal Religious Cult,* & the epigraph to *Conversations*
is from the Syriac Gnostic *Hymn to the Pearl.*

Manufactured in the United States of America
Originally published by The Dial Press in 1971
First published as New Directions Paperbook 406 (ISBN: 0-8112-0590-8)
in 1975
Published simultaneously in Canada by McClelland & Stewart, Ltd.

New Directions Books are published for James Laughlin
by New Directions Publishing Corporation,
333 Sixth Avenue, New York 10014

for Diane, A SLOWER MUSIC

Time runs thru my fingers,
laughter & feathers
against her lips
when I bend to kiss her

She is my wonder, who sleeps
& will not wake for me
but with her tongue brings me bread,
to eat love in a whisper

I know her as we know the poor,
by their houses, measuring
the empty shelves or the glass
thru a door that never closes

Everything is still again
where my love's waiting
the door swings back in place
& the hinges rest

If it is night we are close
if it is morning the sun won't stay hidden
will you wake for me again?
the lost bells cry in sleep

Yes the lost bells cry in sleep

CONTENTS

In the Chippewa "game of silence" the poet makes a deliberate assault on the minds of his audience, working his verbal combinations so as to break their silence by laughter or any similarly loud response.

POEMS FOR THE
GAME OF SILENCE

PROGRAM ONE

1960

The poem is the record of a movement from perception to vision.

Poetic form is the pattern of that movement through space & time.

The deep image is the content of vision emerging in the poem.

The vehicle of movement is imagination.

The condition of movement is freedom.

From
WHITE SUN
BLACK SUN

A LITTLE BOY LOST

They took me from the white sun and they
left me in the black sun, left
me to sleep among long rows of overcoats:
I was a city boy lost in the country, a
wound in my hand was all I knew about willows
Can you understand, do you hear the wide
sound of the wind against the cow's
side, and the crickets that run down my
sleeve, crickets full of the night, with
bodies like little black suns? try as I will
there is only this cry in my heart, this cry:
They took me from the white sun, and they
left me in the black sun, and I
have no way of turning now, no door

THE NIGHT THE MOON WAS A SPIDER

The night the moon was a spider
we ran.
Nobody stayed.
The sky grew as black as your eyes.
It was starting to rain.
Sails in the air
broke loose.
Red sails.
You laughed.
The moon was a spider.
A ribbon of blood reached down
from the sky
to the roof of our house.
Red and black.
We were trying to sing.
It was cold.
In the net of the sky
where the bones were hanging
I saw
what I thought was your face.
The scraping of
wheels over rock
in the dark of the moon.
Begin:
The night the soldiers drove by
I rose from our bed,
my hands bound behind me,
and looked.
You were trying to dream.
An icicle broke from the sky
and entered my heart.
The moon was a spider.

INVINCIBLE FLOWERS

The flowers here are so sad, I could cry.
Not one of them acts like a flower, or carries itself like a flower.
Not one grows red overnight in the sudden anguish of spring.
They lie in wax wrappers and fidget.
Or sometimes, a head peers over a vase, half alive:
they've surrendered.

Colors die out as innocence fades in the eye of the florist.
Adjusting his watch he strides past the roses.
Shouting orders at something—the evening perhaps—he will
        smother the lilies.
Only the ferns will survive his cigars (and then for how long?)
Tulips, asters, begonias, etc. are squeezed in a single dark box
        full of wadding,
sent out every day to hospitals, weddings and graves.
Eternal observers, these silent, terrible flowers.

No! Give me plastic flowers, flowers in granite and ice,
proud flowers cut into monuments, honoring God, the flowers of
        poverty,
flowers formed by the hands of young girls in lofts in the
        Bronx,
cut out of papers in Tokyo, hidden in shells,
flowers pasted on walls in great bunches, painted on bottles, on
        stones, enticing "real bees" to my table.

But sometimes, not meaning to, I find that I forget.
I find that I remember things that are better left forgotten.
Perhaps when it rains in my room,
and the window is open, the sheets are thrown like sand on the
        floor,

and my hand like a falcon is diving on quarries of paper,
I hear (at first in the distance) the sound of a great Flower
crying out loud in the sun.
And the thought of something I would not betray grows wild in
    my heart.
The light is enclosed on each side by the darkness of flowers.

A POEM FOR THE WEATHER

In the eye of my needle
everything sprang into life:
a dog, a town
and an ocean.
Roses grew tigers
and someone spilled rain on my scarf.
Over the moon we could hear
the voice of the president,
clear as a church bell,
simple as ether:

under the oranges,
summer sat without moths.

THREE LANDSCAPES

I
The dark bull quartered in my eye
turns slowly from his herd: the branches
part, and now his grey tongue,
trembling, fights a nest
of adders: stung,
the bloodroot quivers in the earth:
too late he walks along a
pebbled beach, his forehead
(like a grieving moon) against the sea.

II
Tonight the river's warm with
bathers: Christ!
to throw myself against the rain,
be swallowed in its
darkness, like an eyelash.

III
White monks are climbing hills
inside her skull: the
fragile ash of love that falls in sleep,
as in the heart of laurel,
touched by drops of blood: so
too, within the cheek
of silence, beauty dressed in white
steps forth: in silence
forty monks await her on a ridge
of cinders, raising forty
candlesticks against the moon.

THE STATIONMASTER'S LAMENT

I have buried her under a stone
The eagles fly past our house with umbrellas
The grey forms rise in the grass
I have buried her solemnly
Speaking the words that she knew:
And the chairs have stood by my side
The trains have been constant in death

The trains have been constant
The conductors who watered our plants have dropped by:
Nodding their pale Busterkeaton-like heads
The brakemen have played farewells on their cellos
Have rendered their final farewells
And the chairs have stood by my side

The chairs have been constant
The chairs with their arms full of wires were dearer to me
        than my friends
I will never forget them
They and the eagles both loved us (as only our plants had
        before)
They came when I called them
They wept dark tears made of burlap
And stood by my side

I have buried her under a forest
The conductors who walked with her coffin were there
The benches were there with white thermoses turning her sheets
With burning black eyes the telegraph keys called the wind
Now they sleep at her feet
And the brakemen play their farewells

We have paid our farewells with her plants
Where the grey forms were rising commuters climb ramps
        through the night
They throw in their fistfulls of earth and bad dreams
They run to the edge of the night where no one will follow
Past lakes of blue darkness where furnaces holler like bulls
And I sit with the three hundred chairs of my dreams
They have stood by my side
I will never forget them

And the trains have been constant in death

From
BETWEEN

WORDS

Terror of words
positions &
dispositions
around a burning
center
Words on paper
in the wounded light
of trees
& undercurrents
words in uncut bread
in curves of
uncut bread   I come
toward you
in the curve of words
of uncut space
the sudden
movement of our lips
together
with breath itself
a language
Also a language
rising from the earth
our footsteps
speaking
like a dance
our words a dance
of breath of
images the single
image of a sun
burning inside us
as we speak

Words cut through us
in the curve of time
the undercurrents
when we wake together
in the first sun
this is real pain
the words are also
pain
The words are filling
with saliva & the shapes
of trees the words
take shape around a
curve of light   I bring you
what words I know
Words on paper in the
loaves we cut
words are in the sun
& wait
they fall against us
treachery of words
of ashes
falling toward the center
silence born from speech
we draw breath
from silence
uncut space
& silence
footsteps breathing
softly
where we learn to die

WOMEN & THIEVES

The women dream
in blue shadows.

The women dream of
houses & thieves.

Then it's Sunday.
Thieves

search your walls
with red gloves.

This is the terror
of sleep.

A blue passage.
& no one

to summon or heal
till morning.

A SIDE OF BEEF

1
The meat hooks are black, covered
with flies licking
the blood, these black meat hooks

In the air a late fly
hovers: it will find a window
& rest there

& I will find no one:
no one will find us
come closer! sit with me here

The windows are burning

2
The meat hooks are black
with white flies
They are licking them, ah
the black meat hooks

Ah the black meat hooks
the presence of death
in a room where a meat hook
swings from the ceiling

The meat hooks are black
with black flies
They are watching over them, ah
the black meat hooks

3
But listen, won't you?
listen to the blade
as it swings
& the meat hooks

& the black meat hooks
where the sunlight
falls from the ceiling

where the fire burns,
how many animals
come to eat from your hand?

A face cut in two:
in the blood that covers each eye
a black meat hook

4
They come toward where I am
but we are further away
still further
every time they reach us

we are further away
for being here, for watching
the black meat hooks

It is not light enough
to see you, when I look around
your shadow burns

your shadow turns from me,
the meat hook swings around
a further corner

5
& the meat caught beneath a nail
that is a dream,
the meat hooks that are a place
toward which we journey
& a place where the fire burns

& the meat hooks that are black
& that the flies cover
the meat hooks that I watch
alone, without you

feeling the sun against the window
the sea, this cry
from my birth that drowns me
that will leave my body someday
open, waiting for its flies

POEMS FOR THE HELL OF HUNGRY GHOSTS

for D.W.

1

A white rose burns in the center of the garden. What else is there to say? I will stand here coatless & listen to the others talk. Someone complains that he's hungry. But haven't I seen the hungry before? Nothing will concern me tonight. The hungry, the desperate, the mad: what are they beside the charred bones that we leave behind us? Forget them. The black sky still rises over our heads.

2

And the fire dies. The swollen tongue rolls in the mouth, the teeth scrape against each other, a white film rises from the throat. The dying man is on the floor beside us, no longer to be trusted. But wasn't the poison good that we gave him? Eyes throbbing in the withered skull, the whole mind bursting into darkness. What did he ask of you? A little food?

3

(*Tenochtitlan*) The living room is where the ceremony takes place. The chieftain, dressed in the golden skin of his victim, sits by the window & smokes. A clay bowl is on the table in the center. It contains the victim's heart & fingers. A marriage ring glitters in the dish. Lost in thought the chieftain lifts a knuckle to his lips & waits. The meal takes place in silence. Afterwards the bones are gathered in a silver box: he brings them to an altar in the foyer.

4

But Hell is always present. It is with us in the tree that rises skyward like a sword. We climb it slowly, but the blade is sharp: it cuts our legs, our testicles. A wind blows the thin leaves that strike our hands like razors, that slash our eyes & ears. We fall lightly through the darkness where the river waits for us. My mouth fills with vinegar. Upstream, downstream: death is on all sides.

5

Now *I* was hungry too. When the soldiers pulled me from the river I threw myself at their feet. I too became a beggar. But what was the good of it? They were heating an iron crowbar which they put to my mouth: they forced my lips apart with it, then they placed a tiny red-hot ball inside me. Down it went, burning. My tongue, my throat, my chest: a screaming fire. What would be left of me? Day & night, the same. I write these words from Hell.

6

What you are you cannot escape. The fire may make it a little more clean, but the fire is only a reminder. It is like the voices speaking around me. What are the voices speaking around me? They aren't only the dead or those whom I loved, but they are also those whom I hated & who hated me. Because we couldn't touch each other in the darkness or draw close, & because we stood coatless in the garden & only listened, & because hunger & pain had lost all meaning, we lived for what was not ourselves. But that was its own punishment of course: & if you tell me there is some greater punishment I will not believe you: & if you say there is some greater pain I will welcome it gladly.

THE SEVEN HELLS OF THE JIGOKU ZOSHI

THE FIRST HELL: *of measures, where swindlers measure fire*
in iron boxes

How can any of you know
what it feels like
to count coins in Hell

You have the rest of it to keep you busy
Your eyes are troubled enough

But down here
the nights are longer
& the days are senseless
Down here
the rain falls
upside-down
from iron boxes

The smoke inside the narrow room
pulls back
It winds around the bedposts
like a colored cloth
around a leg that's bleeding

Violet & green
with pain

What should we say to our fingers?
Should we remind them
of the cool silk yards
they handled behind counters

The healing lotions
rolled between the palms

Should we tell them that the earth
crawling with black grief
at least was wet

1
2

Blue coins of disaster
are ringing in the night
The distant call of metal birds
is like the rhyming
in bad poems
before your birth

You would not know me now

The fire at my ribs
has emptied me of flesh & words
I stand here with the others
counting
letting the numbers fill my head
An outlaw

1
2
3
4
5

I want to turn aside
but Hell won't let me
Hell is the outraged customer
who slams the cashbox
against my hands

A candle drips
along the sidewalk
Wax covers the windows of a small store
& blurs the sun

A darkness full of crates
through which I walk
thinking of other hells than this

The skin cries under the brand
of intellect
Deceit of numbers
raising questions in the mind
that's helpless
The fevered brow

Smash it to hell
You have a right to it

1
2
3
4
5

The white eye watches
through the window
Where we live is where
we always lived
The sea of death

THE SECOND HELL: *of mortars, where thieves are ground in*
mortars

The thieves the thieves the lovely thieves are no more
The shore is washed by the sea
The sea is combed by the wind
The wind sleeps all day in the chimney
It moves through the house in the evening
It wakes us, it opens a door for the sea
It walks where the thieves walked
It leads us into a night without windows
Comfort me stay with me light of my eyes
The lovely thieves are no more

The thieves are crying
Their voices are crying from Hell
Their tears fill the snow with lost coins
Their tears burn my fingers
My fingers that move through your hair
How gentle your voice is
Respond to them Answer them
Think of the pain they bear in their skin
The thread that runs from their skin to your voice

From your voice to the wind
Respond to them Answer them

The thieves the thieves the lovely thieves are no more
The shadows are silent
The silence has entered your voice
Your voice is asleep in the shadows
Wake again in the night wake again full of fear
Wake to the shadow of death at your window
The ladders that hung from the sky are falling
The thieves are falling their blood is filling the earth
The earth that awaits you
The earth that destroys you
The earth that has stolen your voice

The earth's voice is crying with hunger
A single grave waits for us all
A single stone grinds us to water
The water flows to the sea
The sea is asleep in your voice
Your voice that could flood Hell with tears
That could ease the pain of the dying
But only the thieves cry tonight
They cry where no one can hear them
Their voices cry from the stone
Their voices cry where we sleep without dreams
The thieves the thieves the lovely thieves are no more

THE THIRD HELL: *of excrement, where those condemned for vile actions are eaten by worms in a cesspool*

Do you see them?
Do you see the pederasts in that yellow wetness
crying & turning, raising weak hands
toward the sun, do you hear their voices
fading in the light that dies all around them:
sinking, everything broken, everything covered with mud &
        odors of urine
whirling in the shadow of a cracked moon
dissolving in the dark whirlpool that carries them into the earth?

I see them
I hear their voices, oh I see their pale lips rise for the last time
& hear them scream at the night:
I hear the cries of the small boys on the shore
feet running along the side of the river, hands
outstretched holding sheets of delirious colors
stumbling through soft miles of sand, hunting
the dim horn of the moon in the marshes:
the lost sounds of the pederasts in the turmoil of the third sad
        hell

The doors of hotels in the darkest quarter of the city stand open
I see the men passing through with black satchels
spreading the sheets for the night, covering their moist backs
        with white towels
the managers smile at the guests, the bellboys enter the room
with curved vases, with poisons poured into pitchers, with whips

the size of small birds, with phonograph records that play
      Turkish songs
with powders & perfumes, with glasses for teeth:
I see the priest look back on the stairs (his cassock raised to his
      knees)
& the bats that fly down the halls
& the testicles throbbing like frogs

By morning the river grows calm, the faces
are gone from the windows
Boats come past with long oars pressing the reeds
shapes barely seen in the rushes
      float past their bellies turned to the sun
eyes lost forever, lost in a dawn without voices:
the boys sit stunned in the sunlight
They stir the water with straws
or lean on bare elbows watching the currents

And love? was this love too, this delusion?
The kingdom of hell knows better, will pay them in kind not
      kindness
The kingdom of hell, the white kingdom, the country of worms,
      the defiled
the distorted, the broken, the perjured, the twisted, the maimed
the pathetic mad hungry creatures who clawed after love, the
      deformed
The kingdom of earth was no better

THE FOURTH HELL: *of cruelty, where those condemned for cruelty are tortured by a fiery cock*

They wait forever at those windows
watching me

In greasy shirtsleeves, heavy
lids, blotched faces
Counting the time till food
or stepping over eggshells
in these empty lots

God I'd like to see them all in Hell
the whole damn pack at once!

Turn the gamecocks on them, let
the flaming beaks tear at their hands & mouths
Until the black teeth stand alone

& down their backs
the fire running slowly, eating
the rotted flesh away

Up Broadway, past the
Hell of Twenty-Third Street
walking, watching
the windows red with fire
Skins & furs piled along the curb

Hands reach around me, voices
whisper out of doorways

Camouflaging knives & acids, blue
sweat shining on their cheeks
The colors of disfiguration

Let me go

My eye bursts, the green
pulp trembles from the socket
Falling to the sidewalk
in dark drops

Pain holds a string between us
leading from our open wounds
The tissue that won't heal

It binds us, suffering
& drawn together
Hatred our first link as men
our covenant

Herald Square is empty:
faces rise inside my mind
& track me down
The black sun fills the sky

I know them, they waited
in the light, they watched the narrow point
recede, the flesh drawn back
Fires racing down his belly

Burning into him

their anger, slowly burning
words in, burning life
The cry of sex, dark letters

In the Hell of Times Square
boys bind themselves
to pain: the cock of fire
blossoms, bringing death
into the streets

A golden flower
swollen by the wind

Who cries for pity? let
the cock destroy them, let
the torn night swallow us
& spit us up

The key to Hell is here
A thousand keys

The scars the dark beaks leave
grow slowly, swelling
in the shadow of God's light
that drives us mad

THE FIFTH HELL: *of unclean food, for those who served
unclean food to others*

     The fattened sky
resting at the door of this

          white butchershop
carries the old wounds:
The poor meat stands without skin & streams blood,
it covers flowers & roots in the window
flows in slow rivers under the paws of a cat
The butcher sees me & smiles
          the red steam coating his apron
The breasts of the housewives are heavy with salt

Our looks cross from a distance:
          I feel the grass part
in his smile, the soft paws brushing the earth
Why should this butcher concern me?
Why should I want to run or cry out
          to rise like a river of teeth?
Why should I look so long at those rows of sweet flesh,
the flanks black with flies, the white tiles?

His breath is stirring the hair of these women,
like dry smoke it moves down the aisle
          past the register
          comes to rest on the scales:
Salt & fire, dismemberment, blood, old commitments
marigolds stuffed into jars in the sun
the flesh caving in, the warm center
          Now they come in small groups
to watch the skulls behind glass
the gouged eyes, the hills of flayed bones
the blue despair of the sinews
the soft hairy flesh

The butcher prods the young leaves:

Someday
when the dawn has grown old
we will face each other across the wet roofs
(like the priests of Xipe watching the Spaniards draw in)
And the bones will tell us that life eats life & grows fat
        that we claw at each other
(Have I said enough now? Are you sick enough of this meat?)

        Sitting at tables
stuffing our skulls with the tag-ends of life
we will go on as before
        forgetting
changing flesh into words, words into paper
lying in wait for each other
eating ourselves on this miserable earth
        And if sometimes
we should pass a window
        strewn with flowers & flesh
& the old memory of the old wounds should begin
& the sweet smell stick to our throats:
We will know again
        that image of a dark bull
bathed in its entrails
        a shroud of wild heavy flowers
that draws us to worship in silence
the sorrow of all this poor meat

THE SIXTH HELL: *of women pursued by fire-breathing monsters*

Because she breathed too wildly in the sun
Because the sun had risen for her because it fell into her lap

Because she held a bird between her legs, eyeless, but the face
      still warm, still tender
They have left her

Because sand was covering the factories
Because the wind wiped out the traces of a bridge
Because their throats bled spiders & poppy seeds & wheels
They have left her

Because it was raining when she got there
Because the houses overflowed with broken tiles
Because horses grazed along the river & in the cities fires
      burned in empty stalls
They have left her

When it was over a rain of salamanders washed the suburbs
Magnetos burned her eyelids & the fibers growing from her
      spine
When it was over blue milk bathed the beaches
They have left her

When it was over the living room smelled of submarines &
      death
When it was over her eyes closed to crazy throbbings
      underneath the moon
When it was over the trolleys shattered glass in front of
      convents
They have left her

Sorrow ran down the hills where she bled
Sorrow older than the stones lining the highways older than
      the sea

Sorrow of lions crying from before her birth
They have left her

In the rain in the unlit places where the morning waits on its
        dead
In cemeteries overlooking monstrous cities
In the granular darkness of her womb with its cry of raw
        beginnings
They have left her

In the wake of autos speeding over sunless roads
On anguished nights in resorts in casinos overrun by a chimera
At the blind center of a sundial
They have left her

Now dawn rides the restless ferries out of town
Dawn swallows a city in its hunger, waiting with new blood
        across its lips
Dawn grovels in the minds of those who wait, the lately risen
They have left her

They have left her in the rain where her voice was sleeping
They have sucked the moon & stars from her veins
& have left her, to return to empty offices with windows high
        above the sea
They have left her

They have left her bathed with water-guts & lymph
They have left her with bandages that cry & teeth & open sores
With her shadow eyeless on the shores of Hell
They have left her

Oh shadow risen from an ocean without boats
Oh shadow of lost roads & comets lonely shadow sleeping in the
     wind
Oh shadow of the silence's deep echoes
They have left her

Oh rain of hair oh flower without roots
Oh dark flower of death oh rose of desperation
Oh virgin without fingers oh hands I cannot touch oh to whom
     should I turn?
They have left her

There is no one nothing I can hold: the rain against the steps
This room oppressing me with love, old wounds, the fear
     beginning
Rising, till I cannot stand or walk
They have left her

Till I reach for her: a hairpin on the floor, a shawl
& all the doors are closing where she sleeps
These long mornings without hope or rest, this fever as the
     sunlight falters, as the rain falls down
They have left her

THE SEVENTH HELL: *of smoke, where fire-raisers try in*
                                vain to escape from a shower of hot
                                sand falling from a cloud

The houses of men are on fire
     Pity the dead in their graves

& the homes of the living
Pity the roofbeams whose waters burn till they're ash
Pity the old clouds devoured by the clouds of hot sand
& the sweat that's drawn out of metals pity that too
Pity the teeth robbed of gold
       The bones when their skin falls away
Pity man's cry when the sun is born in his cities
& the thunder breaks down his door
         & pity the rain
For the rain falls on the deserts of man & is lost

If the mind is a house that has fallen
       Where will the eye find rest
The images rise from the marrow & cry in the blood
Pity man's voice in the smoke-filled days
     & his eyes in the darkness
Pity the sight of his eyes
        For what can a man see in the darkness
What can he see but the children's bones & the dead sticks
But the places between spaces & the places of sand
& the places of black teeth
      The faraway places
The black sand carried & the black bones buried
The black veins hanging from the open skin
     & the blood changed to glass in the night

The eye of man is on fire
     A green bird cries from his house
& opens a red eye to death
The sun drops out of a pine tree
      Brushing the earth with its wings

For what can a man see in the morning
What can he see but the fire-raisers
       The shadow of the fire-raisers lost in the smoke
The shadow of the smoke where the hot sand is falling
The fire-raisers putting a torch to their arms
The green smoke ascending
            Pity the children of man
Pity their bones when the skin falls away
Pity the skin devoured by fire
       The fire devoured by fire
The mind of man is on fire
       & where will his eye find rest

A BODHISATTVA UNDOES HELL

> Because he saw the men of the world plough-
> ing their fields, sowing the seed, trafficking,
> huckstering, buying & selling, & at the end
> winning nothing but bitterness, For this he
> was moved to pity . . .

To the figures bathing at the river
Jizo appeared

The sky was full of small fishes
The bodies of the men
twisted in an afternoon
when earth & air were one

With Hell a hard fact
the double lotus

brought the son of heaven
down among us
And the bathers showed their hands
that bore the marks of nails

What Jizo said
was this

Let's bury their lousy hammers
My people
are tired of pain
The world's been crucified
long enough

The rain fell gently on their wounds
The women lugged
big platters of shrimp
to the bathers
when Jizo's diamond
caught the sun

The rest of us
sat at the stone windows
overlooking the river
We saw him climb the hill
& disappear
behind the guardhouse

What he told the guards
was this

Your bosses are men
who darken counsel
with words
But the white sun
carries love
into the world

When Jizo leaned on his stick
the blue lines in his face
were shining with tears
We followed him
into the city
where lilies bled beside a lake

He said

The heart's
a flower
Love
each other
Keep the old
among you

Write the poem
The image
unlocks Hell
Man's joy
makes
his gods

For those who heard him
hatred fell away

We spent the night
with angels
Fishing
in the ponds of Hell

THE JOURNEY BETWEEN SUMMERS

To Robert Kelly & Octavio Paz

dissolution of your names,
two cities

hidden in her lips, a
frightened dust

& the portion of my eye
that still sees

watches morning, this
green light

across the bed.
The mountain leaves us.

Shivers. I
think of

Paris, white
water

& black trees. I
hold her close.

We sleep: the
movement

between poems
is half my life,

the other half
your voices.

A thought. A nerve
detached from sleep,

forcing a passage,
rains

against the further door.
We force it.

Strangers we stand
unknowing

in a stranger's house.
Somos

desconocidos, strangers
to your love.

Yet the same grass holds us,
where you slept we

also sleep, the grass
is warm with your shapes.

With strangers. My body
covers hers. The grass

swarms with old alphabets.
A god once walked here,

bent to your voices.
And when it's dark

on the porch of some
old farmhouse,

because the sky
is that much darker

or hearing the voices
from below the earth

of animals, I form
the letters of your names

in light. Or draw them
from her lips.

It is that still.
Death awaits us

in what's nearest.
Only a voice.

It is enough. It
is enough.

It doesn't last. We
leave this mountain

too. It is enough.
I wait here

& the old woman,
nearly dead across the way

screams. Another name.
I have no voice

to say it. It is
enough, no name to give it

but death, this
radiance

across the room
we move to

as I cup her face,
my hands

reach up to it
& fold

as you would say,
in sleep.

FROM THE COUNTER-DANCES OF DARKNESS

for Robert Duncan

THE DANCES

The penis, this other miracle, enters the dark, the body enters
        the dark & will soon be wed to the darkness—
which of these will keep sight of the heavens, will seek light as
        its first, its only source?
& the root that presses deep in the earth—what does it seek?

. . . .

The myriad roots that turn from the light—into earth, the
        darkness
how does the loss of the heavens sit with them? or their place
        in the total design?

1
The dancers move forward—I am last in the circle, changing
my body, pretending to be with those who had died in the fire
my love a deceit, starting from the lowest level of what I would
        soon become—
fire, fire, the smoke asleep in their golden veins, as with fire &
        blood.

2
Someone to speak to me, someone to answer me where I stand—
your light is a mystery over these hills, twining me, whispering
        through me,
the first rain over my hands as it hurries to touch me—in that
        light
your shadow had yet to appear, it was a conciliation, but
        clearer than that, a beginning.

3

There is a movement in its rooms no longer—
a locket that was shaken by the wind
& a dead body that rests with the other dead bodies—
evening, my shadow touched by the headlights from a passing
        truck
while across the road other shadows cover other dead bodies—
I had forgotten where it began,
I can only remember the ache in your fingers
so cold, so in need of my breath to wake them.

4

As I dreamed my stature (mad dream!) as in the pasture at
        night
among the freaks, the many-headed cattle, loiterers—
that I could match their size—that bewildering bruteness,
could be set apart where I walked to be mocked—
this monster, this debaser, broken & degenerate & eternally
        damned & alone—
only not to be whole—a part of that order, the goad for its
        senseless stars—
not to give life & watch it taken back again—
what wars in a single lifetime! what slow deaths worse than all
        wars!
what bliss as the body dissolves, turns sour, returns to its
        pitiless earth!
does a flower offend you?
does the sun make you cringe that opens every inch of you with
        careless fingers?
for this I had made myself monstrous!

how many others must die to force one moment of doubt to
       your throat?

5

The silence will open—as a hand will open against your hand
though its fingers will not open—or will open only to my breath
       that moves them
or as the wind moves the curtains to show a field, the corner of
       this sky
the corner of your eye that sleeps inside me—
in the shadow of the eaves the trigger spoke, uncoiled the spring
       broke loose,
clouds big with thunder, golden shapes of birds leaped skyward
fell & crushed themselves against my hands—
still others will crush themselves against my hands
& when the dead return, there will be other ways of telling time
& many strange words then—
& there will be a language also—of our own.

6

The existence of the horrible in every particle of air—
among its roots, submerged in droplets—vision!
You were not immune to it—neither at evening with the rain
       still in your hair
nor in the garden at noon—not the first to be spared, to raise a
       cry
against its stars—what imbecile regrets for all your nights of
       silence!
No one had dreamed your pain then—how it would draw the
       fingers back

would drive its roots inside you—muscle & joint, the knot, the
       hard enclosure—death?
Around you the air was suddenly alive—
whole cities full of the "luckless dead"—pavilions—marchers
but your heart couldn't contain it—like the universe it shrank,
       became your fist
abandoned in the rain, the odor clings to it—
& there are places in the dark where no light enters,
where a hand moves slowly through the silence, on the wall
a pressure that was like the earth, took color from it—
your shadow in my blood—for we were someone's dream of
       vengeance.

7

Not in a meadow—the dead who are dead & the dead who will
       be dead
& the bull driven to a slope below the house, a dark, terrible
       shadow
& your darker shadow, the moon—
for this we delayed, for the night, just started, to end
for time to lose all dimension—only the kiss at your throat, the
       warm touch of you
curve of my blood through yours—but the dead were with us
       from the start
it was a circle, a habit of repetition,
first sensed in the breaking of bread, the heifer's dance into life
the mother cow swollen her bag hanging down to the earth
also a root through the earth—all swollen, all broken
you woke to it under the moon, but in darkness—
in darkness it had begun—in darkness, in darkness it will be
       ended.

PROGRAM TWO

1964

1) I will change your mind;

2) any means (= methods) to that end;

3) to oppose the "devourers" = bureaucrats, system-makers, priests, etc. (W. Blake);

4) "& if thou wdst understand that wch is me, know this: all that I have sd I have uttered playfully—& I was by no means ashamed of it." (J. C. to his disciples, *The Acts of St. John*)

From
SIGHTINGS
& FURTHER
SIGHTINGS

SIGHTINGS I–IX

He hides his heart.

•

A precious arrangement of glass & flowers.

•

They have made a covenant between them, the circumstance of
      being tried.

•

Who will signal you?

•

It doesn't open to their touch though some wait where it rests.

•

Try sleep.

•

The emblem perhaps of a herd of elephants—as signal for a
        change in weather.

•

Animal.

•

A pigeon dreaming of red flowers.

II

A hand extended, or a page.
The witness.

•

In the way we eat—it is this that moves me, to be guided by it.

●

Whiteness.
Her shadow & my own.
For color.

●

That leaves a number less than one.

●

For balance: snow or horses.
(Seals).

●

How we had rested (the question).
By elevations (the response).

●

A finger growing from a finger:
Hell in glass.

III

The lie, beginning, persists with us.

●

Measure of a day, bracken, green leaves, etc., a place to find
      refuge, to return.

●

But how many before I scream?

●

Not in your throat, I mean; the selfishness of wax.

●

A bigot.

•

Take yes for an answer; they will have arrived here long before
      your setting forth.

•

The outline of my hand on black paper.

•

My eye on black paper too, to form a clock.

•

A male-shaped womb—of darkness before the birth of light.

IV

1.   Wait!

2.   A throw of the dice.
     A blue paper.

3.   This marks the presence of certain minerals.

4. At midday. The blaze of day in the sky.

5. Would he pause for you, bending? raise to his lips what was yours? so careless, my eye falters; careless.

6. This violence of new preoccupations.

7. A twisted wire.
   Ink.

8. And for those who watch the snow, a slow decline.

9. For this she had chosen to dwell among you; let her, for our peace.

V

Description of an eye stone.

•

That began it, not water at first but another sort of light & much darker.

•

At best an abandonment.

•

The skyfall rose over her legs, a violent cry of mosses near the
      point of juncture.

•

Salt.

•

Then the bodies fucking, of men & animals, drew his soul into
      the seed, & in that moment sperm touched egg, & he
      was born.

•

A torch.   A door.
A road.   A mirror.

•

But that which weeps is the mind.

VI

1. The earth shudders under the rain.

2. A hand.
   Five fingers.

3. Milkweed; was it that?

4. They add in rows.

5. Beginning from the waist, slip downwards; force a smile.

6. Perhaps a dish.
   A cup.

7. Horse   grey   knot
   fallen   throat   of-blood.

8. One thought, a thousand movements.

VII

Division of the work, by light.

•

It is a table.
We stand around it.
There are chairs too, a candle.

•

And others, walking in the courtyard, dream of us, each step
        another key.

•

A tree.

•

This makes a watersound.

•

I could not plot the difference; time, I mean.

•

Or find her, let her nipples swell against my lips.

•

A glass jar
shatters, the floor
is white,
full of black wheels,
like a clock.

                                                                    VIII

He waited in the room below.
He struck the hammer.

●

That concludes a phase: her orange sections, oddly, to the life.

●

Make a counterproposition.

●

Money.

●

In sleep, a granular deposit.

•

Let her hands reach out, disclosing in the light, a paper mask.

•

Exposing in the night, your hair.

•

A black bear, motionless against the sea.

•

Where did they come from?
(Silence.)

•

The calendar: But he had died before!

IX

Allotments.
Shut.

•

A pale ellipse; this would spell some kind of root, a summoner.

•

A summer ayre.

•

They call the nerve diseased.
Her FIre?
Sacred bangles,
& yet the leg won't burn.

•

Then spurn her.

●

Desire, oddly, for a well.

●

Shut.

●

All light we will become, be gathered.

FURTHER SIGHTINGS

2 x 7

"The Old King"

for Leir, in Hades

The Old King (i)
painted his face—
a hand as border.

The Old King (ii)
eye of Horus
& of the hawk.

The Old King (iii)
harps, timbrels
to his touch.

The Old King (iv)
a striped mirror—
a green shell.

The Old King (v)
another
guardian.

The Old King (vi)
who strikes the moon
to contain it.

The Old King (vii)
divides the cut
circle, gems.

FURTHER SIGHTINGS

The Sabbath Queen (i)

waited in woods
a mooncalf
would have fled

The Sabbath Queen (ii)

who held a rooster
to the light
& danced with it

The Sabbath Queen (iii)

of fat
the portion tithed
the margin

The Sabbath Queen (iv)

black candles :
on her grave :
the sin of onan

The Sabbath Queen (v)

a fresh wax
container
of milk & seed

70

The Sabbath Queen (vi)

drew metals from
the earth
in spite of sleep

The Sabbath Queen (vii)

of the bride's journey
to light, o
this canopy in hell

FURTHER SIGHTINGS

(1st Set)

1. A white shadow in Hell.

2. Like Hell's beauty
   in mirrors—
   that you will never reach.

3. In the season of smiles,
   Hell was waiting.

4. Why does the hermaphrodite beckon?
   Is it that Hell lurks there?

5. The breathing of the lion is Hell.
   The insouciance of certain birds is also Hell.

(2nd Set)

1. Hell's direction,
   circular,
   inscribes a circle.

2. I knew Hell in their voices
   & in the rhythms of certain trees,
   an indolence across the sea
   at dusk, & periwinkles.

3. What began in hope ends in sorrow—
   as Hell will always wake in your kiss.

4. There were three women he loved:
   one, as Hell spoke, moved him,
   while the others slept.

5. Hell of numbers, pale,
   reflecting water,
   in distrust of all eyes.

(3rd Set)

1. Two bodies struggling—Hell.
   A touch deferred—also Hell.

2. We were speaking of Hell all night.
   Had the sisters heard us?
   She was alone, I kissed her & turned aside.
   You have brought me pictures from Hell.

3. Hell opened before their headlights—
   but against that light, the other Hell.

4. Gold—or the pollen set behind her eyes.
   Hell's emblems.

5. And the bride must rest from light—
   test & measure of her resting, for the peace of Hell.

FURTHER SIGHTINGS

(1st Set)

1. I am the man who held the keys.
   I asked you to forgive me.
   I was the first to be insistent & the last to leave.

2. I vomited
   I didn't come there often.
   I was eager & alive.

3. I was not the least among them.
   Once I was.
   Once I remember being in a poor position.

4. I applied for membership.
   I was sad.
   Then I thought no longer to go on living.

5. I turned from you & offered you my keys.
   You turned beside me & offered your position.
   I had turned against them.

(2nd Set)

1. I will make no promises.
   I had made electricity before then.
   I would dream of making light.

2. I do it now.
   I do not do it often.
   I do not do it but I care.

3. You asked me to write my name but I had never learned it.
   I insist on pain.
   I walk & run in stages.

4. I was sometimes coarse to you.
   I had no patience.
   I stiffened.

5. I believe in free education & other values.
   I was starting to feel princely.
   Tell me where I erred.

                                                    (3rd Set)
1. I had the same chances as any other slave.
   I hold a hand up.
   Once I thought it was January, it was really June.

2. Do I understand you.
   Does the key I give you fit your mind.
   My love for you is senseless.

3. I am what you see I do not see myself in you.
   I had learned to reason.
   I had no necessity for friends.

4. I wore a shirt.
   I welcome those who welcomed me.
   I am sincere.

5. I am the man who held the keys.
   I will make no promises.
   I had the same chances as any other slave.

A Note on SIGHTINGS:

The measure of SIGHTINGS involves the creation of an equivalent area-of-silence around each phrase or succession of phrases in the poem.

To read these, let the spaces between phrases (as marked by the points at the left-hand margin) represent a silence equal or proportionate to the duration of each succeeding phrase.

In FURTHER SIGHTINGS & SIGHTINGS IV & V, where the numbers & titles take over most of the compositional function of the points & spaces, it is only necessary to make a noticeable pause between the numbered sections.

From
A STEINBOOK
& MORE

A VALENTINE, NO A VALEDICTORY
FOR GERTRUDE STEIN

She be blesst.
Morning.
Open to touch.
Morning.
No key but a possible movement.
Of the foot.
Exchange.
Morning.
This woman who speaks without breath has opened the
ring for me.

LORCA'S SPAIN: A HOMAGE

Beginning with olive trees.

Shadows.

Beginning with roosters.

Crystal.

Beginning with castanets & almonds.

Fishes.

This is a homage to Spain.
This mists dogs.
This silences rubber.
This is Saturn.
Beginning with yellow.

Eclipse.

Beginning with needles.

Insomnia.

Beginning with baskets.

The Moon.

Who is naked? The imagination
(wrote Lorca) is seared.
This is a homage to water.
Beginning & end.

SOME NOTES FOR A NEW SERIES OF POEMS
TO CELEBRATE THE AMERICAN
REVOLUTION (1776–1976)

for Diane Wakoski

1.

Before beginning I have a few things left to do.

And before beginning.

I have a place to find for being tired, I have some hard work
& to stretch my legs, I have persuasion as a last resort.

Before beginning candles.

Before beginning the tired feeling after oratory & the nights
after oratory.

Before roads which have nothing to do with where they're
going.

Is someone pleased. A question.

I have a question & beginning the count to count the dead.

The testimony is wasted effort.

Likewise music.

2.

Retreat.   Make love.   Build cities.

Open baskets.   Shovel quick stones.

Mark the compass.   Bathe.   Be open.

Find a better place to bathe.   Run.

3.

Every Sicilian is a clown.

Every Jew is a manager.

Every Negro is catastrophic.

Every Irishman is every.

Every effort to be framed is dull.

Every well is dry.

Every promise is a better day.

4.

The king was the last to arrive.
He had a terrible headache.
They gave him aspirin.
The taste was hard for him to believe.
The water was harder.
The goats were locked in the mirror.
The more the merrier.
Good morning, neighbors.
His breath smells sweet to everybody.
Smile for the king.

5.

She has written a poem in which there are no bodies but only points of radiant light.

She watches the lights move & understands only that her own eyes are moving.

She pretends to be the first woman to speak in an uncertain voice.

She opens her hands in front of her face & sees the lights falling down.

She is ready for snow now that it's over.

6.

She is two steps further along the road but by tomorrow she will just have started.

She is not Betsy Ross & has no stars to cut into shapes but only lights.

She is not the first queen to wear silk.

She is never a queen herself but knows the others by a kind of introduction.

She is thanked twice but she fails to respond.

7.
She calls herself the mother of your country.
She is self-proclaimed.
The others who are self-proclaimed stare at her in wonder.
She is seldom there.

8.
Empress & tree.
Tree & pit.
Or war.
Or simply war.
Or simply watermelons.
Each side begins war.
Tree & pit.
Empress & watermelons.
& often memories.
Or war.
Or simply war.
Or simply watermelons.

9.
They are hurting each other.
They are smiling.
They are saying that they are in love & offer you a place to
turn from it.
They are the color of ice.
They are best cleansing.
They are again without speech & from this they gain power.
They survive without blame.
They are blameless.

> **How**
> **she**
> **would**
> **hurt**
> **him, a narrative.**

(1) They were of course relieved by it. Of course the moon was in the opposite direction.

(2) And again tomorrow.

We do this cautiously.

Again we do it then we please each other.

(3) She is free.

And she is happy.

A narrative

to

please.   (1) By pleasing.   (2) Í beg them for attention. (3) We were of course relieved to be there.   (4) The sun is popular in those old stories.

(5)

Then he tells us to ask as many questions as we want.

(1) We ask his shape.

(2) We ask three particular directions.

(3) We ask unaccountably.

(4) We ask from friendship.

(5) We ask how she would hurt him.

(6) We ask for the moon.

And therefore.

Therefore is very cruel.

Therefore is physical.

Therefore is eager & wanting.

Therefore receives.

Therefore grieves.

In sections.

Then by sections therefore.

A narrative.

He answers   (1) vertical
                    (2) red white & blue
                    (3) turning from me
                    (4) one friend more
                    (5) alive & alive
                    (6) beyond all compasses.

A lesson.

Now a lesson.

Now a narrative & showing cunning.

Shut.

And therefore.

(1) A certain space.   (1) A temperature.   (1) An act of healing.

(2) A loss of place. Reclining. Therefore.

There or therefore.

(3) Surprisingly.

(4) & (5) Identical. A message. Less a hand.

(6) A narrative. Beyond.

Beyond a narrative.

It is better to be on with it.

By pleasing.

No wisdom but beyond a narrative.

He was left without his verbs & nouns.

But helpless.

RED EASY A COLOR

1.
Red a color.
Red an object in space surrounded by a color.
Like color.
Or further like a color.
In & green.
To flourish.
Their sense of history.
& time.
Too many times to be too many people.

2.
Red a fantasy.
Color. Objective colors cool.
Colors fading.
Loss of the space between two colors.
What the woman gives is red.
A sense of satisfaction.
Colors.
Of a loss in space.

3.
Of a sense of red.
The face become an image.
Hands an image.
White & yellow.
Yellow.
Red.
A sense of color.
Now a second sense of color.

4.
A heavy body. Red.
Red images & set in circles.
The red of circles.
& animals. To sleep
Sleeping below red circles.
No colors of.
Colors of their flesh.
With red.
America.

5.
Red easy a color.
Make & manufacture. Stamp
A color. Easy.
The return of merchandise.
Directions. Unfold
& open. Press the tube & wait.
Red ointment.
Red in movement on a hand.
Red wound. Sex
Red. Delicious
& alive.
Red life beginning.
Easy. Red. A fantasy.
A sense of red. Her color
Is alive & cures.

From
CONVERSATIONS

"But through some cause they marked that I was not their countryman, & they ingratiated themselves with me, & mixt me drink with their cunning, & gave me to taste of their meat; & I forgot that I was a king's son, & servd their king. I forgot the Pearl for which my parents had sent me. Through the heaviness of their nourishment I sank into a deep slumber."

CONVERSATION SIX

What's in a name?
(Sounds.)
How many sounds is what I want to know.
(I never count sounds.)
Do you count strokes?
(No I count resolutions.)
Count one now.
(One two three four five six seven eight nine ten eleven twelve thirteen.)
That sounds like a long resolution.
(Yes resolutions are forever long.)

CONVERSATION SEVEN

I am building a machine.
(Let me see it.)
Here it is.
(Where does this piece go.)
Behind this piece.
(Where does a window go to look at the machine.)
It goes alongside the machine.
(Is the machine going to be standing on this floor.)
No in this field.
(I want to write my name in the middle of your field.)
My field is a machine.
(Can I cross it.)
No.
(I want to sit on your machine then.)
No; machines can break.

CONVERSATION TEN

They will rise up & murder you.

(I am dead already.)

They will move libraries into your churches & trade your daughters to the Moors.

(I only ask a fair return.)

They will defile you with money their lewd fingers will never let you sleep.

(I welcome their attentions.)

The children of Ham & the children of Canaan will be at each other's throats.

(I believe you.)

Have you no fear that your loins will grow feeble that there will be no tallow for generations to come?

(I have never understood this.)

They will live on the fringe of your cities their faces will be like yours & they will kiss you like brothers.

(Then I will rise up & murder them.)

CONVERSATION THIRTEEN

I was talking to him.
(Yes.)
He was talking to me.
(Was he.)
We were talking to each other about the weather & also because because of talking.
(Was he talking to you because of talking.)
No the weather is innocent.
(The weather is fine.)
But the weather is best to be talking about not only the weather of course.
(Were you talking about tomorow.)
No we were talking tomorrow.
(He talks I talk & you talk.)
Then everybody will soon be talking.
(Yes.)
Tomorrow.
(Yes.)
It is better to have no regrets then everybody is fine.

CONVERSATION FIFTEEN

I wanted something to eat.

(I wanted nothing.)

I wanted a place for resting & another place for the pleasures of sleep.

(I wanted the joys of charity.)

I wanted the weather.

(I wanted you.)

Were you hungry?

(No.)

Were you remarkable?

(I was remarkable & was never hungry.)

I wanted hands.

(I wanted to be free of touch.)

I wanted my hands to be tied to the side of your body.

(I wanted your body to be tied to the side of my house.)

I was an animal & was never free.

(I wanted the vindication of the just.)

From
THE
GORKY POEMS

"I like the heat, the tenderness, the edible, the lusciousness, the song of a single person, the bathtub full of water to bathe myself beneath the water.

"I measure all things by weight.

"I love my Mougouch. I hate things that are not like me & all the things I haven't got are God to me."

ARSHILE GORKY

THE PIRATE (II)

This man was a pilgrim.

For what, for
a journey?
What kind of a journey?

For ice.

The snowheaven turns into
stone, the snow-
garden vanishes. Under
the sea
who had dreamed it?

Who? Who breaks rocks
moves an inch
either way, who eats iron?

What a country of robots.

The way of the Lord
is through ice.
This is the Lord's Day.

And That?

A silver brilliance
cold
hard
painful
blue.
A true flag of colors.

No, a paperbag.

The shadows in a paperbag
that no one sees.
The highpitched laughter no one hears.

The ice no one feels.

What men!
What stone in their voices!
What glass in their blood!
What iron! What flesh!
What bright eyes!

This stone, this iron
in a dream
still worse when no one dreams it.

THE DIARY OF A SEDUCER

Fat. Fat. Fat. Fat. Fat.
This is the forbidden kingdom.
This is Shape
That balloons & is a power
In the light.
O Don Roberto. O lovely Don Roberto.
You have become an idol my love for you is no longer no
longer that I love you O Don Roberto O lovely Don Roberto.
Don Roberto farewell.
Don Roberto in the morning sitting among his birds &
singing.
Don Roberto fiesta.
Don Roberto clear fields in autumn he is riding the tar road
into Tivoli.
Fever Don Roberto.
Claw Don Roberto.
Talon into haunch of rabbit Don Roberto.
Don Roberto with a candle & a granite head.
With eyebrow of Zukofsky
& a woman's body Don Roberto.
Priestess in the guise of Don Roberto.
Feeble Don Roberto.
Angel angel Don Roberto.
Bearded & taloned Don Roberto.
Where will the ecstasy end Don Roberto.
Or the numbers cease
if ever the numbers will cease Don Roberto.
Answer body for body Don Roberto.
Name of Don Roberto.
Color color & ensign of Don Roberto.
Shemhazai Don Roberto.

Azazel Don Roberto.

Barakel Don Roberto.

Kawkabel Don Roberto

Ezekeel Don Roberto.

Arakiel Don Roberto.

Samsaweel Don Roberto.

Seriel Don Roberto.

O lovely Don Roberto. Farewell.

In the shape of your body farewell.

In the shape of the man's penis & of the woman's farewell.

In the shape of the moon & of lunacy farewell.

In the shape of your seven lost companions

& of the pressure of your wand moving towards my eyes
farewell.

Farewell Don Roberto.

We do not know Don Roberto.

We do not sit in the silence of the road to hear Don Roberto.

We have not been pleased to say Don Roberto.

Do I say Don Roberto.

I say sometimes I say sometimes I say Don Roberto.

& will sometimes say Don Roberto.

Don Roberto who is ghost of Don Roberto whose hidden
name is hawk.

O Don Roberto. O lovely Don Roberto.

THE WATER OF THE FLOWERY MILL (II)

for the Angel

He is blood, himself
the killer
is where the sun goes down.

Will he flex his arm, will
the fingers
narrow, make a fist around
the bauble, crush it?

Dust is his.

The entry into light
the courtyard
white with marble veins
& suicides
the perfect edge for sleep.

Count the numbers.
Call the monster green
the little eggs
the wind cups
everything is far from him.

His blood is far from him

& makes a circle, poisons
where it falls
the country dies from it.

Sweet smelling flesh
sweet dung
sweet tumor in the eye
sweet bauble:

as the fish are lanterns
upon waves

& light the sea for him.

THE BETROTHAL

How they began it. Dead bodies
moved in the flowerbed, a finger stopping & turning, showing
a page & an ocean, a longboard covered with stars. *In the
great night
my heart will go out*, will be scooped from me, swept thru the
water
follow the plane's route, a place
where boats meet like lovers
in couples, the heart of the diamond, the cyclotron's heart,
its spaces
cleaving me, leaving me dead.
I was dead.
Who steps from the sea to meet me?
Another dead body, a heart like a cucumber
cold, green, in the ice-covered room, receiving my heart
the taste of my blood in her mouth.
Her dead mouth.
The passage into her darkness, a gutter
a rainpassage
country of clouds & the blue lips of women.
A hand slides under his shirt. He grows hard. The dancers
forget where the light is
& fall, the dancers forget
they falter
their hands break the glass
a finger stopping & turning, showing
a skull. Lift the hammer
& over your head lift the icecap.
Smash thru the air. The air freezes &
freezes against you

covers your hair & your teeth, slits your gums, draws bile thru your nose.

To the sound of drums, the cry of walruses, the beating of a heart
not my own
to the beating of a heart not my own
I was turning.
In the trunk I was turning.
Among crushed hats I was turning.
Under a crushed sun I was turning.
I turned with the sun. A faucet
was turning
black water spillt from a glass.
Starting & turning, returning
& starting. A penny.
A seal.
An umbrella.
An American flag.
A wishbone.
A derrick.
A place.
We called it a place by subtraction.

AGONY

5 x 7

for Gorky in Paradise

Agony (i)

Hands.
Hands open.
Hands with grapes.
Behind hands.
Hands behind hands.

Agony (ii)

Under hands hands.
Under.
Agony & glass.
& pressures.
Of pipes & roots.

Agony (iii)

First trust in me.
First love.
A ring is glass & is.
My roots.
My agony.

Agony (iv)

Weave a cloth.
By weaving.
& by weaving a cloth.
Weave by thirds.
Minus one & two thirds.

Agony (v)

Open one.
Open me.
Open one by one.
Open three.
Open agony.

Agony (vi)

Of where a wheel falls.
& a ring.
& where a ring is glass.
& is.
A ring is glass & is.

Agony (vii)

Weave tomorrow.
Yes.
Yes.
Yes.
Weave lines.

THE ORATORS (II)

1
Be no stranger to
Air. Be
Killer, the golden

Delivery.
Be as you see it.

Do
Not. But
Be.

& be guardian.

2
Be tooth.
Seal apart.

Be sentinel.
Vibrate.

Be vapor
Contain.

Be cave.
Blossom.

Be bush.
Murder.

Be moth.
Be.

Be aureole.
Essence.

Ardors.
America.

3
To be
It
With touch.
Oh.
I touch.
Your hands.
That
Touch
My face.
Let
Be.
Turn from
Touch.
Be
Far
By
Turning.
Twice.
Or in a thrice.
Or by turning.

4
Be me who
Blesses.
Suffer. Destroy.

Be certain.

Merge a particular picture
Blossom. & open
This surface to clouds.

Be orators.

CHILD OF AN IDUMEAN NIGHT

1

I, the fat god
I, the good gardener   (p. klee)

Deposit me in your heart
& go to war gaily
Be a singer to Philistia
& carry an American flag
to the border

O Jerusalem
O city of mechanics

Covered with hair of fire
Beard against beard
A row of tigers stands there

Be holy, I say
Write on water
Become the first architect, be
Father of your race

& let men fuck your beard

2

I, tallow
I, voice of holocaust
I, crystal

I, open door

I, decimal
I, winter solstice

I, willow
I, dancer
I, wind-udder

I, parchment
I, avatar
I, shoe

I, harmonica
I, tongue of doves
I, emblem

I, regiment
I, globus
I, pustule

I, tooth
I, tumescence
I, father of tractors

I who swallow the dead
I who die
I who shit with the jackal

I who swell

3
They walk, eyes
In chest

Believing their peace
Their warm days
They burrow
They call me
Master
They say & we dream
Master master
Candle with how many wicks
Destroyer
Worshipper
God of the Tsars
Old father
Old language the father spoke
& wrote it in brass
& that was the testament in brass
& there were other testaments
& iron
& still other testaments
& still other old languages
& I wallowed
& I bathed in the heavy water
Master master
I was firm & substantive
I showed myself
I labelled this part hair
& that part tendon
& I reached between my legs
I grew fat
I became the father of my race
My wide hips in the dust
My heart
Was with the children

Believing
Their peace, their warm days
& still other testaments
I bellowed
I spat
I made thunder
I was first before the Senate
Someone called me
Master
Master
Child of an Idumean night
Possessor
Murderer
First to sit on the stone
To ride the locomotive
& be lost
& to proclaim the kingdom
& to be lost again
& swollen again
& fattened without a sense of repetition
But "made fat with fatness"
In the dust
My wide hips in the dust
& I reached between my legs
& I wallowed
& I bathed in the heavy water
My throne
My sweet light
My substance
This tsar did many good things
Though he was no father

CHARRED BELOVED

Fire night.
Falling.
In threes.
Winter weather.
Sand's eye.
Heaven.
Makes a place for it.
Sea comb.
Hard.
Webs of tears for it.
Hard.
Not ribbons.
Not light ribbons not to stand as blue blue thermometers by skylines no that's as days.
Makes a place for it.
In threes.
That's as days.
Makes a place for it.
To say to make a place for it covers me over discovers a leaf no a life not a life in me.
Not ribbons.
A life in me.
But not blue.
But not blue & over.
Not blue but red.
But not red.
But not blue & red.
But blue & red but.
Over blue & red.
But yellow.
A sea comb.

In threes.
But in threes.
In threes.
But in yellow threes.
In yellow but in threes.
But falling.
A door is first.
A yellow door is in threes.
But a first door.
In threes.
Call a trivet.
A trivet.
Around the mouth.
And gums.
It's an egg hour.
Moistens.
Not an egg.
But elements brought under skylines not light but to measure
it to measure by what beyond salt salt measures.
Beyond salt measures.
In threes.
Elements in threes.
Beyond measures.
This makes a web.
Beyond threes.
But beyond what a web is.
A web is.

PORTRAIT OF MYSELF WITH ARSHILE GORKY & GERTRUDE STEIN

AG   I do direct the night.
                    I do.
                    & walk through it.

GS   The sea is cool.
                    The boats are dominant.
                    The idea of algebra is lost.

                    Almost nowhere is worthwhile.

JR   My own care my trade plied that eases occupa-
tions.
                    Nowhere at ease.

AG   Not because peace is with us.

GS   Nowhere more mechanical.
                    Nowhere function.
                    Nowhere at ease.
                    Nowhere at ease.

                    Nowhere more at ease.

JR   Turn turn & beg exceptions.
                    Scold the sea.

AG   I can make a hurried exit I put propellors to rest.

GS   Not because I scold.

JR   I who am saint.

I who am not saint.
I who am am not saint.

I salvage.

GS, AG   Do you.

JR   I scold the sea.
I try turning.
Spurning remembering.

GS, AG   Do you.
Do you.

JR   I can establish covenants & lease ground for foreclosers
& tell how many steps are needed.

GS   Can you.

JR   I can figure to Wednesday.

GS   Must you.

JR   I can begin with a number & end with 33.

GS   Must you.

JR   I can never be more certain than when I was.

GS, AG   Must you.
Must you.

116

JR	I can miss Miss Ann I prepare her belly for lust.
GS	Am I white.
AG	A color.
GS	I am ball. Am I.
JR	Yes & the motion of wanting to be cool.
JR, AG, GS	Before law. Before water. Before water the dove.
GS, AG	Please warm us.
JR	Warmly. Warmly.
GS	Fish warmly.
AG	Fish & designs.
GS, AG	Desires.
JR, AG, GS	Manage an oracle. Manage a meal. Manage an oarlock.
JR	& a preparation to be already drowned.

A Note on *THE GORKY POEMS:*

The poem "Charred Beloved" goes back to 1962, when Milton
Resnick inspired me to look again at Arshile Gorky's work. In the
aftermath of that look came *Sightings I–IX* & the start of *Further
Sightings*, & I'm tempted to believe that their structure of suspension
in time & space isn't unrelated to Gorky's own workings. The remain-
ing Gorky poems were written in 1964–1966 & bear diverse & often
loose relationships to Gorky's paintings, titles, poems, or to my "sense
of Gorky." But they aren't *about* these things, for the last thing I
would have learned from Gorky is to write poems about Gorky. There
is finally no key to the relationship, & an attempt to construct one
would only be misleading. If the poems connect with the paintings it's
only as Gorky's own *Diary of a Seducer* does with Kierkegaard's
essay of that title—there, as often here, a naming after-the-fact. Per-
haps it's always those things that can't be *really* defined that are the
most interesting elements in any relationship. A matter of conver-
gence.

PROGRAM THREE

1968

I think of myself as making poems that other poets haven't provided for me & for the existence of which I feel a deep need.

I look for new forms & possibilities, but also for ways of presenting in my own language the oldest possibilities of poetry going back to the primitive & archaic cultures that have been opening up to us over the last hundred years.

I have most recently been translating American Indian poetry (including the "meaningless" syllables, word distortions & music) & have been ex-

ploring ancestral sources of my own in the world
of Jewish mystics, thieves & madmen.

I believe that everything is possible in poetry, &
that our earlier "western" attempts at definition
represent a failure of perception we no longer
have to endure.

FROM
A SHAMAN'S
NOTEBOOK

THE ANNUNCIATION (*by Marpa*)

•

a man born from a flower in space a man
riding a colt foaled from a sterile mare
his reins are formed from the hair of a tortoise

> a rabbit's horn for a dagger he
> strikes down his enemies

a man without lips who is speaking who
sees without eyes a man without ears
who listens who runs without legs

the sun & the moon dance
& blow trumpets

a young child touches
the wheel-of-the-law

> which turns over

•

: secret of the body
> : of the word
> > : of the heart of the gods

the inner breath is the horse of the bodhisattvas

whipped by compassion it
rears it drives the old yak
from the path of madness

124

A SHAMAN CLIMBS UP THE SKY

Altaic, Siberia

•

The Shaman mounts a scarecrow in the shape of a goose

above the white sky
beyond the white clouds
above the blue sky
beyond the blue clouds

this bird climbs the sky

••

The Shaman offers horsemeat to the chief drummer

the master of the six-knob
drum he takes a small piece
then he draws closer he
brings it to me in his hand

when I say "go" he bends
first at the knees when I
say "scat" he takes it all

whatever I give him

•••

The Shaman fumigates nine robes

gifts no horse can carry
that no man can lift &
robes with triple necks

to look at & to touch
three times: to use this
as a horse blanket

                     sweet

prince ulgan

you are my prince
my treasure

you are my joy

••••

Invocation to Markut, the bird of heaven

this bird of heaven who keeps
   five shapes & powerful
   brass claws (the moon

has copper claws the moon's
beak is made of ice) whose

   wings are powerful &
   strike the air whose tail

is power & a heavy wind

markut whose left wing
   hides the moon whose
      right wing hides the sun

      who never gets lost who flies
   past that-place nothing tires her
who comes toward this-place

126

in my house I listen
for her singing I wait
the game begins

falling past my right eye landing
here
on my right shoulder

markut is the mother of five eagles

————

The Shaman reaches the 1st sky

my shadow on the landing
I have climbed to (have reached
this place called sky
& struggled with its summit)
I who stand here
higher than the moon

full moon my shadow

    •
————

The Shaman pierces the 2d sky

to reach the second landing
this further level

look!

the floor below us
lies in ruins

At the End of the Climb: Praise to Prince Ulgan

three stairways lead
to him three flocks
sustain him PRINCE ULGAN!

blue hill where no hill
was before: blue sky
everywhere: a blue cloud
turning swiftly

that no one can reach:
a blue sky that no one
can reach (to reach it
to journey a year by water

then to bow before him
three times to exalt him)
for whom the moon's edge
shines forever PRINCE ULGAN!

you have found use for the hoofs
of our horses you who give us
flocks who keep pain from us

                    sweet

prince ulgan

for whom the stars & the sky
are turning a thousand times
turning a thousand times over

LILY EVENTS

Arnhem Land, Australia

(1)   A man & woman looking for lilies.

(2)   All the people going down to look for lilies.

(3)   Mud taken up looking for lilies.

(4)   Washing the lilies in the water to remove the mud.

(5)   Washing themselves off after the mud has got on them.

(6)   Lilies in a basket.

(7)   Walking from the lily place "to go look for a dry place to sit down."

GARBAGE EVENT

Dayak, Borneo

1. Pigs and chickens feed on the grass in an inhabited area until it is bare of grass.

2. Garbage is added to the area.

3. The participants defend the "abandoned beauty" & "town-quality" of the environment against all critics.

SAMPLE DEFENSE:

Critic. This place is dirty.
Answer. It is filthy.

Critic. Why don't you clean it up?
Answer. We like it the way it is.

Critic. Garbage is unhealthy.
Answer. The pigs feed better in it.

Critic. It breeds mosquitoes.
Answer. There are more mosquitoes in a jungle.

GIFT EVENT II

Kwakiutl Indian

Start by giving away different colored glass bowls.
Have everyone give everyone else a glass bowl.
Give away handkerchiefs & soap & things like that.
Give away a sack of clams & a roll of toilet paper.
Give away teddybear candies, apples, suckers & oranges.
Give away pigs & geese & chickens, or pretend to do so.
Pretend to be different things.
Have the women pretend to be crows, have the men pretend
to be something else.
Talk Chinese or something.
Make a narrow place at the entrance of a house & put a line
at the end of it that you have to stoop under to get in.
Hang the line with all sorts of pots & pans to make a big noise.
Give away frying pans while saying things like "Here is this
frying pan worth $100 & this one worth $200."
Give everyone a new name.
Give a name to a grandchild or think of something & go & get
everything.

SEA WATER EVENT

Arnhem Land, Australia

The tides of the ocean & the floods are danced; certain birds &
animals are included.

FURTHER SIGHTINGS: "KUNAPIPI"

Arnhem Land, Australia

(1st Set)

1   The musk of her
          red-walled vagina
      inviting coitus

2   Her skin soft like fur

3   She is shy at first, but soon
    they laugh together

4   Laughing-together
    Clitoris
    Soft-inside-of-the-vagina

5   Removing her pubic cloth
        opening
            her legs
       lying between them &
    coming

6   & copulating for a child

7   Fire   Fire
    Flame   Ashes

8   firesticks &
    flames are
    flaring

sparks
are flying

9   Urination
Testes
Urination

10   Loincloth
(red)
Loincloth
(white)
Loincloth
(black)

(2nd Set)

1	"penis"	incisure	incisure
	penis	semen	penis

2   Semen white like the mist

3   with penis erect
the kangaroo
moves its buttocks

4   step by step
she walks away from coitus
her back to them

5   the catfish swimming
& singing

6 the bullroarer's string

7 The nipples of the young girl's breasts protrude—
  & the musk of her vagina—

8 creek
  moving

  "creek"

9 mist covering
  the river

10 cypress branches
  cypress cone
  seeds of the cone

SHAKING THE PUMPKIN: Some Songs from the Society of the Mystic Animals, translated with the assistance of Richard Johnny John.

Seneca Indian

CAW CAW THE CROWS CAW CAW

(1)

the crows came in

(2)

the crows sat down

TWO MORE ABOUT A CROW, IN THE MANNER OF ZUKOFSKY

(1)

Yond cawcrow's way-out

(2)

Hog (yes!) swine you're mine

A SONG OF MY SONG, IN THREE PARTS

It's off in the distance.

●

It came into the room.

●

It's here in the circle.

```
hiiiiiiiiiiiiiiiiiiiiiiiiiiiiiiiiiiiiiiiiiiiiiiiiiiiiiiiiiiih
e                                                          e
e                                                          e
e        THREE WAYS TO SCREW UP                            e
e                                                          e
e     ON YOUR WAY TO THE DOINGS                            e
e                                                          e
e                 THREE WAYS                               e
e                                                          e
e                                                          e
hiiiiiiiiiiiiiiiiiiiiiiiiiiiiiiiiiiiiiiiiiiiiiiiiiiiiiiiiiiih
```

    (1)   I fell down.

    (2)   I got lost.

    (3)   I lost my bucket.

A SONG ABOUT A DEAD PERSON
—OR WAS IT A MOLE?

                    YOHOHEYHEYEYHEYHAHYEYEYHAHHEH
oing thru the big earth
                    YOHOHEYHEYEYHEYHAHYEYEYHAHHEH
                                            I went thr
                    YOHOHEYHEYEYHEYHAHYEYEYHAHHEH
                        I was going through the big earth
                    YOHOHEYHEYEYHEYHAHYEYEYHAHHEH
                        I went thru this big earth
                    YOHOHEYHEYEYHEYHAHYEYEYHAHHEH
                                    I was going thru the
                    YOHOHEYHEYEYHEYHAHYEYEYHAHHEH
        I went thru this big earth
                    YOHOHEYHEYEYHEYHAHYEYEYHAHHEH

                    YOHOHEYHEYEYHEYHAHYEYEYHAHHEH
rth
                    YOHOHEYHEYEYHEYHAHYEYEYHAHHEH

                    YOHOHEYHEYEYHEYHAHYEYEYHAHHEH

                    YOHOHEYHEYEYHEYHAHYEYEYHAHHEH

WHERE THE SONG WENT WHERE SHE WENT
& WHAT HAPPENED WHEN THEY MET

the song went to the garden	(heh heh heh)
the song poked all around the garden	(heh heh heh)
she went to the garden	(heh heh heh)
she went to the garden	(heh heh heh)
she went like crazy in the garden	(heh heh heh)
that's where she went	(hah hah hah)

YO OH HEYA YAH
YO OH HEYA YAH
YO HO HEYA YAH   We made a mistake in this song
YO OH HEYA YAH
YO OH HEYA YAH

YO OH HEYA YAH
YO OH HEYA YAH
YO OH HEYA YAH   We'll have to straighten it out
YO OH HEYA YAH
YO OH HEYA YAH

YO OH HEYA YAH
YO OH HEYA YAH
YO OH HEYA YAH   This time we'll do it right
YO OH HEYA YAH
YO OH HEYA YAH

TWO SONGS ABOUT FLOWERS & WHERE
I WAS WALKING


```
P L E N T Y   O F   F L O W E R S
h                                 h
i                                 e
i        PLENTY OF FLOWERS        e
i                                 e
i        WHERE I'M WALKING        i
g                                 g
h                                 h
W H E R E   I ' M   W A L K I N G
```


```
C A T   T A I L S   A R E   G R O W I N G
h                                         h
i                                         e
i          CAT TAILS ARE GROWING          e
i                                         e
i           WHERE I'M WALKING             i
g                                         g
h                                         h
W  H E R E   I ' M   W A L K I N G
```

A Note on SHAKING THE PUMPKIN:

Minimal poetry. Extensive use of a restricted number of non-semantic vocables. Words few & far between. Traditional sacred poetry with a strong play element, especially where used for renewal rather than curing—or, as Seneca singer Richard Johnny John explains it: ". . . but if everything's alright the one who says the prayer tells them: I leave it up to you folks & if you want to have a good time, have a good time!" Oral elements translated by visual (paginal) equivalents. To read sounds aloud, follow your own play-principle to wherever it takes you.

THE FLIGHT OF QUETZALCOATL

Aztec

•

Then the time came for Quetzalcoatl too, when he felt the darkness twist in him like a river, as though it meant to weigh him down, & he thought to go then, to leave the city as he had found it & to go, forgetting there ever was a Tula

Which was what he later did, as people tell it who still speak about the Fire: how he first ignited the gold & silver houses, their walls speckled with red shells, & the other Toltec arts, the creations of man's hands & the imagination of his heart

& hid the best of them in secret places, deep in the earth, in mountains or down gullies, buried them, took the cacao trees & changed them into thorned acacias

& the birds he'd brought there years before, that had the richly colored feathers & whose breasts were like a living fire, he sent ahead of him to trace the highway he would follow towards the seacoast

When that was over he started down the road

•

A whole day's journey, reached

THE JUNCTURE OF THE TREE
(so-called)

                    fat prominence of bark
                    sky branches

I sat beneath it
saw my face/cracked
mirror

An old man
                    & named it
                    TREE OF OLD AGE

thus to name
it to raise stones
to wound the bark
with stones

to batter it with
stones the stones to
cut the bark to fester
in the bark

                    TREE OF OLD AGE

stone patterns: starting
from the roots they
reach the highest leaves

•

The next day gone with walking
Flutes were sounding in his ears

                    Companions' voices

He squatted on a rock to rest
he leaned his hands against the rock

                  Tula shining in the distance

: which he saw he
saw it & began to cry

he cried the cold sobs cut his throat

      A double thread of tears, a hailstorm
      beating down his face, the drops
      burn through the rock
      The drops of sorrow fall against the stone
      & pierce its heart

& where his hands had rested
shadows lingered on the rock: as if
his hands had pressed soft clay
As if the rock were clay

The mark too of his buttocks in the rock,
embedded there forever

The hollow of his hands preserved forever

               A place named TEMACPALCO

●

To Stone Bridge next

water swirling in the riverbed
a spreading turbulence of water

: where he dug a stone up
made a bridge across
               & crossed it

•

: who kept moving until he reached the Lake of Serpents, the elders waiting for him there, to tell him he would have to turn around, he would have to leave their country & go home

: who heard them ask where he was bound for, cut off from all a man remembers, his city's rites long fallen into disregard

: who said it was too late to turn around, his need still driving him, & when they asked again where he was bound, spoke about a country of red daylight & finding wisdom, who had been called there, whom the sun was calling

: who waited then until they told him he could go, could leave his Toltec things & go (& so he left those arts behind, the creations of man's hands & the imagination of his heart; the crafts of gold & silver, of working precious stones, of carpentry & sculpture & mural painting & book illumination & featherweaving)

: who, delivering that knowledge, threw his jewelled necklace in the lake, which vanished in those depths, & from then on that place was called The Lake of Jewels

•

Another stop along the line

> This time
> THE CITY OF THE SLEEPERS

And runs into a shaman

Says, you bound for somewhere honey

Says, the country of Red Daylight know it? expect to land there
probe a little wisdom maybe

Says, no fooling try a bit of pulque brewed it just for you

Says, most kind but awfully sorry scarcely touch a drop you
know

Says, perhaps you've got no choice perhaps I might not let you
go now you didn't drink perhaps I'm forcing you against
your will might even get you drunk come on honey drink
it up

Drinks it with a straw

> So drunk he falls down fainting
> on the road & dreams &
> snores his snoring echoes very far

& when he wakes finds silence
& an empty town, his face
reflected & the hair shaved off

> Then calls it
> CITY OF THE SLEEPERS

●

There is a peak between Old Smokey
& The White Woman

Snow is falling
& fell upon him in those days

> & on his companions
> who were with him, on
> his dwarfs, his clowns
> his gimps

> > It fell

till they were frozen
lost among the dead

The weight oppressed him
& he wept for them

He sang

> The tears are endless
> & the long sighs
> issue from my chest

Further out
THE HILL OF MANY COLORS

which he sought

Portents everywhere, those
dark reminders
of the road he walks

•

It ended on the beach
It ended with a hulk of serpents formed into a boat
& when he'd made it, sat in it & sailed away
A boat that glided on those burning waters, no one knowing when
    he reached the country of Red Daylight
It ended on the rim of some great sea
It ended with his face reflected in the mirror of its waves
The beauty of his face returned to him
& he was dressed in garments like the sun
It ended with a bonfire on the beach where he would hurl himself
& burn, his ashes rising & the cries of birds
It ended with the linnet, with the birds of turquoise color, birds
    the color of wild sunflowers, red & blue birds
It ended with the birds of yellow feathers in a riot of bright gold
Circling till the fire had died out
Circling while his heart rose through the sky
It ended with his heart transformed into a star
It ended with the morning star with dawn & evening
It ended with his journey to Death's Kingdom with seven days of
    darkness
With his body changed to light
A star that burns forever in that sky

SOUNDINGS: From THE 17 HORSE-SONGS OF FRANK MITCHELL

THE 12TH HORSE-SONG OF FRANK MITCHELL (BLUE)

Key: wnn N nnnn N gahn   hawuNnawu   nngobaheegwing

Some are & are going to my howinouse baheegwing hawuNnawu
    N nngahn baheegwing
Some are & are going to my howinouse baheegwing hawuNnawu
    N nngahn baheegwing
Some are & some are gone to my howinouse nnaht bahyee naht-
    gwing buhtzzm bahyee noohwinnnGUUH

Because I was (N gahn) I was the boy raised Ng the dawn(n)
    (n) but some are & are gowing to my howinouse baheegwing
& by going from the house the bluestone hoganome but some are
    & are gone to my howinow baheegwing
& by going from the house the shahyNshining hoganome but some
    are & are gone to my howinow baheeGWING
& by going from the swollenouse my breath has blown but some
    are & are going to my howinouse baheegwing
& by going from the house the hohly honganome but some are &
    are gone to my howinow baheegwing ginng ginnng
& from the place of precious cloth we walk (p)pon (N gahn) but
    some are gone to my howinow baheegwing hawunawwing
with those prayersticks that are blu(u)(u) but some are & are
    (wnn N) gahn to my howinouse baheegwing
with my feathers that are b(lu)u but some are & are going to my
    howinouse baheegwing
with my spirit horses that are b(lu)u but some are & are going to
    my howinouse baheegwing
with my spirit horses that are blue & dawn but some are & are gone
    to my howinow baheegwing nngnnng
with those spirit (hawuN) horses that are bluestone (nawu) but
    some are & are gone to my howinow baheegwing

with those hoganorses that are bluestone but some are & are going
to my howinouse baheegwing
with cloth of ever(ee)ee kind tgaahn & draw them on nahhtnnn
but some are & are gone to my howinow baheegwing
with jewels of ever(ee)ee kind tgaahn & draw them on nahhtnnn
but some are & are going to my howinouse baheegwing
with hoganorses of ever(ee)ee kind to go & draw them on nahhtnnn
but some are & are going to my howinouse baheegwing
with sheep of evree(ee)(ee) kind tgaahm & draw them on
nahhtnnn but some are & are going to my howinouse baheeg-
wing
with cattle of every kind (N gahn) to go & draw them on nahht-
nnnn but some are & are going to my howinouse baheegwing
with men of evree(ee)(ee) kind tgaahn & draw them on nahhtnnn
but some are & are going to my howinouse baheegwing
now to my howinome of precious cloth in my backroom Ngahhnn
where Nnnn but some are & are going to my howinouse
baheegwing
in my house of precious cloth we walk (p)pon (N gahn) where
Nnnn but some are & are going to my howinouse baheegwing
& everything that's gone before (mmmm) more we walk (p)pon
but some are & are going to my howinouse baheegwing
& everything that's more & won't be (be!) be poor but some are &
some are gone to my howinow baheegwing
& everything that's (nawuN) living to be old & blesst (bhawuN)
some are & are going to my howinouse baheegwing
because I am the boy who goes & blesses/blisses to be old but
some are & are going to my howinouse baheegwing hawu-
Nnawu N nngahn baheegwinnng

Zzmmmm are & are gone to my howinow baheegwing hawuNnawu
  N nngahn baheegwing
Zzmmmm are & are going to my howinouse baheegwing hawu-
  Nnawu N nngahn baheegwing
Some are & some are gone to my house now naht bahyeee naht-
  nwinnng buht nawuNNN baheegwinnng

THE 13TH HORSE-SONG OF FRANK MITCHELL (WHITE)

Key: nnnn N N gahn

Some're lovely N nawu nnnn but some 're & are at my hawuz nawu
    wnn N wnn baheegwing
Some're lovely N hawu nnnn but some 're & are at my howinow N
    wnn baheegwing
Some're lovely N nawu nnnn but some are & are at my howzes
    nawu nahht bahyeenwing but bahyeesum nahtgwing

NNNOOOOW because I was (N gahn) I was the boy ingside the
    dawn but some 're at my house now wnn N wnn baheegwing
& by going from the house the wwwideshell howanome but some
    're at my howinow N wnnn baheegwing
& by going from the house the darkned hoganome but some 're at
    my house N wnn baheegwing
& by going from the swollen hoganouse my breath has blown but
    some 're at my house N wnn baheegwing
& by going from the house the hloly hoganome but some 're at my
    house N wnn N wnn baheegwingnnng
& from the plays of jewels we walk (naht gahn) (p)pon but
    some 're at my howinow N wnn baheegwing
with prayersticks that are white (nnuhgohn) but some 're at my
    house N wnn baheegwing
with my feathers that are white (mmm gahn) but some 're at my
    house N wnn baheegwing
with my spirit horses that are white (nuhgohn) but some 're at my
    house N wnn baheegwing
with my spirit horses that are white & dawn (nuhgohn) but
    some 're at my house N wnnn baheegwing
with those spirit horses that are whiteshell nawuNgnnnn but
    some 're at my house N wnn baheegwing
with those howanorses that are whiteshell nawu but some 're at my

howinouse wnnn baheegwingnnng

wiiiingth jewels of every kind d(go)nN draw them on nahtnnn
   but some 're at my howinow N wnn baheegwing

with cloth of every kind d(go)nN draw them on nahtnnn but
   some 're at my howinow N wnn baheegwing

with sheep of every kind d(go)nN draw them on nahtnnn but
   some 're at my house N wnn baheegwing

with horses of evree(ee)(ee) kind d(go)nN draw them on
   nahtnnn but some 're at my howinow N wnn baheegwing

with cattle of every kind d(go)nN draw them on nahtnnn but
   some 're at my howinow N wnn baheegwing

with men of every kind d(go)nN draw them on nahtnnn but
   some 're at my house N wnn baheegwing

in my house of precious jewels in my back(acka)room (N gahn)
   wherennnn but some 're at my howinow N wnn baheegwing

in this house of precious jewels we walk (p)pon (N gahn) where
   nnnn but some 're at my house N wnn baheegwing

& everything that's g(h)one before mmmmore we walk (p)pon
   but some 're at my howinow N wnn baheegwing

& everything that's more (   ) won't be (be!) be poor but some're
   at my house N wnn baheegwing

& everything that's now & living to be old & blesst nhawu but
   some 're at my howinow N wnnn baheegwing

because I am the boy who blesses/blisses to be old but some 're at
   my house N wnn baheegwing

Zzmmmm 're lovely N nawu nnnn but some 're & are at my how-
   inouse N wnn baheegwing

Zzmmmm 're lovely nawu N nnnn but some 're & are at my house
   N wnn baheegwing

Zzmmmm 're lovely N nawu nnnn but some are & are at my howzes
   nahht bahyeenahtnwing but nawu nohwun baheegwing

158

NOTE. The soundings presented here are the scores for my almost final translations of the 12th & 13th of seventeen Navajo "horse-songs" in the blessingway of Frank Mitchell (1881–1967) of Chinle, Arizona. Their power, as with most Navajo poetry, is directed toward blessing & curing, but in the course of it they also depict the stages by which Enemy Slayer, on instructions from his mother Changing Woman, goes to the house of his father The Sun, to receive & bring back horses for The People. The 12th Song marks the point in the narrative where Enemy Slayer contemplates returning home with his father's horses & other good gifts, the 13th where he imagines how beautiful they'll be when actually arrived there. Color in this pair of poems shifts from blue to white, melody remains constant.

With the help of ethnomusicologist David McAllester I've been attempting "total translations" of all 17 horse-songs, accounting not only for meaning but for word distortions, meaningless syllables, music, style of performance, etc.; &, since translation at no point is mere reproduction, even the music isn't free from changes. The idea never was to set English words to Navajo music but to let a whole work emerge newly in the process of considering what kinds of statement were there to begin with. As far as I could I also wanted to avoid "writing" the poem in English, since this seemed irrelevant to a poetry that reached a high development outside of any written system.

Under the best of circumstances translation-for-meaning is no more than partial translation. Even more so for the densely textured Navajo. To present what's essentially a sound-poem, a *total* translation must distort words in a manner analogous to the original; it must match "meaningless" syllables with equivalents in our very different English soundings; it may begin to sing in a mode suitable to the words of the translation; & if the original provides for more than one voice, the translation will also. Does in fact in the final recorded version as I come to it.

In all this what matters to me most as a poet is that the process has been a very natural one of extending the poetry into new areas of sound. Nor do I think of the result as poetry plus something else, but as *all* poetry, *all* poet's work, just as the Navajo is all poetry, where poetry & music haven't suffered separation. In that sense Frank Mitchell's gift has taken me a small way towards a new "total poetry," as well as an experiment in total translation. And that, after all, is where many of us had been heading in the first place.

From
NARRATIVES &
REALTHEATER
PIECES

A FIRST NARRATIVE

He is King.
He matters.
He is King.
He forgives.
He is King.
He is King.
He attends a wedding.
He is King.
He attends a decision.
He attends.
He attends.
He dances.
We see.
He is King.
We siphon.
The inheritors dance.
He matters.
He is King.
We attend a wedding.
He is King.
He is King.
He forgives.

PRAISES OF THE BANTU KINGS (1–10)

1.

I escort.
I go with the dead I don't escort myself.
I was foolish someone else was wise.
I was a lion but had never stretched my claws.
I have no father & no mother.
I remained.

2.

I was the rain's child the rain comes from the east & drizzles.
I am a rain that drizzles.
I soaked some old men without hair.
I am the bed the dead will sleep on.
Sometimes I kept busy once I was looking for a place to cross.
I am the lion's grandson.
I was angry later I roamed their forests.
I am your king.

3.

I was a tree that lost its leaves.
Am I dead?
My skin is hard now only some twigs are left for burning.

4.

I am the one my name is.
I wouldn't let them bury me.
Tomorrow I will visit someone else.
I killed the king & all his children.
I killed the man who owned the island.
Once I killed his brother.

5.

I love.
I overrun the country.
I am awarded lands & people.
I was scornful of their goats & sheep.

6.

I was like a lion in the forest.
I had never been afraid of witchcraft.
I killed my victim then I ate his prick.

7.

I am the rummager.
I dug out lily bulbs.
I searched for siftings of the corn.
I was hunger in a conquered land.

8.

I am beautiful & light-skinned.
I am rain.
I carried the dead children like a stretcher.
I was the road through the cemetery no one could escape me.
I fought buffalos & strangers.
I despised their smalltown ways I only live among the great.

9.

I was a marksman.
I was skilled.
I was the husband of my wife.
I wore my shirttails up.
I sported a goatee.

10.
I dwellt among the crooked.
I was taught.
I straightened up.

FURTHER PRAISES (1–5)

1.
I was your king but suffered for it.
None of my kinsmen suffer more.
I was the "firewood" & injured those who held me.

2.
I was like a mushroom that appears & rots.
I heard the graves rejoicing for their dead.

3.
Someone called me The Maned Lion.
I was a river that buries the dead land.
Once I was a rotten branch a bat's weight breaks.
I was sand covering the hills.

4.
I was lightfooted.
I was heedless through nights of revolution.
I murdered on all sides of me.
I was like a drum I was a drum's voice in the night but sleeping.
I watched the poor rise up against me.
I slaughtered the guards who crossed the lake.

5.
I was the lustful woman.
I wanted a throne of husbands in my name.
Soon I would watch the world with many eyes.
Its kings look small to me.

PRAISE POEMS FOR THE OLD COALITION

1.
He was wise.
He was jewish.
He was philanthropical.
He was interested in sofas.
He withdrew & held back.
He is one of our friends.
The stories he tells you have an insistence all their own.
He is moving back & forth back & forth between here & some
    other location.
He is most respectful at sunup.
(Most respectful & mostly at sunup.)
(As we like to say.)
We hear of him.
This is good he tells us referring to the items at hand.
He was less willing as a young man.
He is the subject of a sentimental biography.
He wears tight collars but keeps the buttons loose.

2.
He said he was a fool.
He beat his breast.
He bit his fingers.
He bent over & let men kick him in the ass.
He smiled.
He giggled.
Some men giggled with him.
He heard them giggling.
He was remorseful.
He was last.
He knew when he had had enough.

"NERO" FROM *THE LIVES OF THE CAESARS*

When he staged "The Fire"
also a ballet performance by certain young Greeks
& simultaneously opened the baths
but refused the titled "Father of his Country"
Nero, not satisfied with the passion he felt for his mother
raped the Vestal Virgin Rubria.
And this was because of his youth
& a wild beast hunt in the circus:
that was when he shaved his chin for the first time
presided at shows of this sort
planned only two foreign tours
likewise expelled from the city all "food of the gods."
A naturally cruel heart
ugly omens were voted him:
he actually raced four-camel chariots!
& the password he gave the colonel on duty was
"The Best of Mothers."
He had reached the age of 17.
Giving Claudius a lavish funeral
Nero watched from the top of the proscenium
a Roman play by Afranius called "The Fire"
& occupied the hindquarters of a hollow wooden heifer
(he early developed a taste for it)
wearing masks
would address the judges,
played a flute,
on one occasion fractured a praetor's skull.
Clearly the true Nero
because one of his games
(from noon 'til midnight)
was to drop the bodies down sewers:

a turban party, yes
a rose banquet.
Also forced noblewomen,
cruised past brothels
pretending,
tried to turn Sporus into a girl by castration
with stones & broken bottles.
Gradually Nero's vices gained the upper hand.
A rather amusing joke:
the passion he felt for his mother
("The Best of Mothers" the password
he gave the colonel on duty)
now lasted from noon till midnight
was notorious.
Nero practiced every kind of obscenity:
skins of men & women in the same litter
incest with Agrippina
("the best of mothers")
he imitated the screams & moans of a girl being deflowered.
Snow-cooled water.
Feasts from noon till midnight.
Artificial lakes.
A handkerchief.
A rain of flowers, bracelets, sulfur water.
1000 assorted birds daily.
Pearls, paintings, slaves.
Ceilings of fretted ivory.
City tenements.
The state of his clothes every time they rode in the same litter.
He also had men at work on a covered bath
& condescended to remark:

"Poisoning!
the food of the gods!
now at last
I can begin to live like a human being!"
Jeers & catcalls.
Antidotes.
Escape.
"I really must get back to Baiae."
At last he tried it on a pig:
the screams & moans of a girl being deflowered
& showed equal generosity to his monkey-faced banker.
Agrippina to be killed:
handling her arms & legs, discussing their good & bad points:
Now mother may come & kiss my national resources.
A cough mixture.
A comet.
The baths which he had built.
The Fall of Illium.
Orestes the Matricide.
Oedipus Blinded.
And "The Fire" a Roman play by Afranius
in which the actor playing Icarus
while attempting his first flight
fell beside Nero's couch & spattered him
with blood.

REALTHEATER PIECE TWO

An open area outdoors, preferably the courtyard of a church or other religious structure. The audience sits on all four sides on long wooden benches. In the center is a deep hole (high enough for a man to stand in) covered with a wide wooden grating; near it a small table with various implements: scissors, knives, cleaver, ribbons, paper flowers, etc. To further prepare the setting, cut down a number of good-sized trees & plant them firmly in the performance area; to these are brought domesticated animals, such as goats & sheep, which are hung alive from the branches. The trees may also be decorated with birds & ribbons, & with ornaments of gold & silver.

Action One

The audience receives long, richly colored gowns, distributed by male attendants wearing short white gowns & otherwise unadorned. The members of the audience remove their street clothes & put on the long gowns.

Action Two

The attendants set fire to the trees.

Action Three

When the trees have started burning, a group of five men enters. They wear white like the attendants but drawn tightly across their chests & hanging down to their feet. They are bareheaded (heads preferably shaven) except for one, The Leader, who wears some kind of exotic headdress such as a turban or a mitre. The Leader carries a baby's rattle in his right hand, an oldfashioned hurricane lamp in his left hand. The four others carry (1) a metal cooking pot, (2) a miniature plastic Christmas tree, (3) a large lady's fan, & (4) the left hand of a store mannikin. At a signal from The Leader, the attendants choose a volunteer from the audience & lead him (or her) to the center of the performance area. The five men place their implements on the ground in front of the table, then use the ribbons, paper flowers & scissors to adorn the volunteer. Once he is adorned, The Leader helps him climb into the hole, over which the attendants put the wooden grating back in place. The Leader remains beside the hole, while the other four lead the audience in singing a miscellany of songs, preferably church hymns like *Gladly the Cross I'd Bear*.

Action Four

A bull, bound with heavy ropes & profusely adorned with (real) flowers & gilded leaves, is brought into the performance area. The attendants position the bull above the wooden grating. The Leader picks up knives & cleaver from the table & begins gashing the bull in a number of places so as to allow the blood to flow onto the grating. The volunteer in the hole now turns his face up to receive the blood. He must make sure that the spurts of blood fall on his head, clothes & body. He must lean backwards to soak his cheeks, his ears, his lips & his nostrils. He must let the wet blood pour over his mouth & must open his mouth eagerly to drink it. At any time he chooses, The Leader cuts the bull's throat & lets the full torrent of blood cover the volunteer. *Action Four* ends when the bull stops bleeding.

Action Five

Remove the dead bull, open the grating & lift out the volunteer, who will come out drenched & dripping, covered with blood from head to toe. Have him return to his place in the audience, which the attendants & the five men lead in reciting the following: BE OF GOOD CHEER, SEEING THAT THE GOD IS SAVED: FOR WE TOO, AFTER OUR TOILS, SHALL FIND SALVATION.

Action Six

Repeat the preceding events with other members of the audience until all have been soaked in blood. If the trees & animals stop burning, the theaterpiece is to be halted immediately & continued the next day. If there aren't enough bulls available, rams or goats may be substituted. A child, preferably male, may also be substituted, but only where there is little danger of interference by the police.

From
POLAND/1931

for Paul Celan

"*. . . And I said, 'O defiled flock, take a harp, & chant to the ancient relics, lest understanding perish.'*"

E. DAHLBERG

my mind is stuffed with tablecloths
& with rings but my mind
is dreaming of poland stuffed with poland
brought in the imagination
to a black wedding
a naked bridegroom hovering above
his naked bride   mad poland
how terrible thy jews at weddings
thy synagogues with camphor smells & almonds
thy thermos bottles thy electric fogs
thy braided armpits
thy underwear alive with roots o poland
poland poland poland poland poland
how thy bells wrapped in their flowers toll
how they do offer up their tongues to kiss the moon
old moon old mother stuck in thy sky thyself
an old bell with no tongue a lost udder
o poland thy beer is ever made of rotting bread
thy silks are linens merely thy tradesmen
dance at weddings where fanatic grooms
still dream of bridesmaids still are screaming
past their red moustaches poland
we have lain awake in thy soft arms forever
thy feathers have been balm to us
thy pillows capture us like sickly wombs & guard us
let us sail through thy fierce weddings poland
let us tread thy markets where thy sausages grow ripe & full
let us bite thy peppercorns let thy oxen's dung be sugar to thy
        dying jews
o poland o sweet resourceful restless poland

o poland of the saints unbuttoned poland repeating endlessly the
        triple names of mary
poland poland poland poland poland
have we not tired of thee poland no for thy cheeses
shall never tire us nor the honey of thy goats
thy grooms shall work ferociously upon their looming brides
shall bring forth executioners
shall stand like kings inside thy doorways
shall throw their arms around thy lintels poland
& begin to crow

THE KING OF THE JEWS

Is a stranger. Is
Sharp. Cries
For fish. Is wanting
A wristwatch.

A poultice. One
Bathes. One intrudes
On the Nightwatch.
One steals.

Catch him. He slips
From your nets. Anoint
Him. The father of weights.
Brother of Edom.

One is a practical man.
One protects. One
Gathers. The table is set.
Find platters.

Find ostriches. Hair
Is refinement.
For thieves. For widows.
A stitch is copper.

One cuts. Makes fingers
That button. He
Suits us. Soon
He is fed.

He is heavy. One
Sings for him. Bathes
In his room.
One counts sheets for him.

Is a steward. Is
Dull. Begs
For soup. Is wanting
A hatband.

One steals. One adds numbers.
He testifies. What
Is a number past one.
A number.

SATAN IN GORAY

A Homage to Isaac Bashevis Singer

1
Sect.
Avert sect.
Avert to wash bellies.
Sect.
Avert sect.

2
Worship.
Womanly.
Towns & Towns.
Tones.
Witness.
Witness & Witness.
Woman redeemed

Woman redeemed woman redeemed.

3
Crutches.
Crutches cockcrow.
Crutches cockcrow Jews.
Crutches impure.
Crutches impure cockcrow.
Crutches Jews.

4
Drinking.
Drinking in devil.
Prayers.
Prayerful.

5
Messiah.
First a holiday malice.
Abyss.
Ark bares Levi.

6
Sabbath.
Sabbatai Zevi.
Sodom Sodom.
Sodom Sodom.

7
Marriage bed marriage bed.
Brittle.
Marriage breasts.
Marriage breasts bristle.
Match me.
Onan.
Again.
Pederasty.
In Three.

8
Fat yes fat yes fat yes idol. Fat yes fat yes fat yes idol.

9
Something is Presence.

10
Holy Muhammed.

11
Pass over.
Pass over.
Pass.
Pass.
Pass.
Pass.
Pass pass.   (G. Stein)

Pass water.

12
Lilith a red head.
Jest nudgingly.
S & Z & S & Z. S & Z & S & Z. S & Z & S & Z. Selah.

THE BEADLE'S TESTIMONY

The boy who throws the ball
A jewel of a boy
His coat down to his feet
Earlocks flying

He will grow up to sell candles
Will eat a dog
& thrive on fat cigars
He will bless his mother too

Yes we are simple people
Yes we drive carts
& work with shit
Sometimes we study

Sometimes a fish in the hand
Sometimes charity
Eros is the Warsaw banker
Spain is far away

Kansas City is also far away
Where did our love go?
I have two hands & only one wallet
I want to speak to you about it

Cities & Jews
Walls & what is behind a wall
A temple sometimes
Sometimes a shining diesel locomotive

Sometimes charity
A boy's shadow on the wall
A jewel of a boy
He will grow up to sell candles

He will bless his mother too

SOAP (I)

The lonely. Sliding
between my hands
A sorrowful island
he dreams of small birds in fragments above his head
& smeared windows
misted eyeglasses
something white floating in a tumbler
lips drinking
remembering a silence white as soap
like rubbing out a name
"the man who writes his name
                        on the beloved's belly"
knows it
what does the man know
hiding from a name?

Answer: "the place where it was hidden"

wax. Sweet
scent
an open skylight
soap
a hand against the tap, palm flat
delight of using soap
he opens papers
sometimes he throws away the ribbon
& picks his nose
Soap in all his orifices
he says, Someone
is clean
Even the doorknob smells of soap

SOAP (II)

Will the man who gets clean love his neighbor?
Yes the facts are apparent yes the facts
Live on in the mind if the mind lives on
"I have no right to another man's business
& it makes me sick"
When Meyer fell asleep in his chair, his wife shouted DON'T
    TOUCH MEYER!
The sugar at the bottom of his cup was brown & hard
Twice a month he had the hairs clipped from his nose
& thanked his barber
(He had sold him shaving soap the day before)
Selling soap to the pious
Calling it *zeyf*
Saying: *ah shtick zeyf*
Or saying: *ah shtickeleh zeyf* (dim.)
Theirs was a business between friends
& meant lying
But the tips of his fingers smelt good to him
Women admired it
The books on his shelf were in a language he couldn't understand
So he began to make little songs
& to stuff his pockets with little bars of soap
"Children, eat omelets
"Children, when the chamberpots are empty the great bear comes
    at night
"Children, there are other values in this life"
Yes said the voices in his dream yes
Sang the voices to the man who sold soap
& was ticklish
But where will the road end, do the voices
Tell you where the road will end

Do they lead you to a new town where the people aren't clean?
"I have no right to another man's business
& it makes me sick"
There were always towns like that

THE MOTHERS

1
scandal, too hard to bear
but kept in her mind
from girlhood   it returned
& hung around the bed
somebody's mouth was always going
words in the old tongue
language of the simple people of our town
there ought to be a book
if someone would ever learn to write with light
& burn it in my heart
that was the way we learnt our history
but forgot it
learnt to unscramble simple sentences
& as a girl husht it up

2
mothers first
& dancers in love with misfortune
together we sat
together we told the bushes the names of our loves
a spy?
a squadron of guards from the palace?
a dirigible back of the lake?
all is secret, sing the mothers
all is innocent
& draws a white circle
behind their eyes
the circle starts to swell   moistens
& leaves a trail of fat
how beautiful, she says

3
she has their desire to be always in love
always respectable
as if prosperity were the name of a town
or of a house in the town
& had no windows
"doomed to old age they withered"
went the song   the secret was out
there will be no sun from this day forward
no more numbers to add up
or coins embedded in the risen dough
all is done, sing the mothers
all is forgiven
& has no book of its own written in light
& no town

PORTRAIT OF A JEW OLD COUNTRY STYLE

visitor to warsaw
                    old man with open fly
            flesh girls could suck
                        mothers would die to catch sight of
sometimes would pass your door
                    his song was
            a generation is a day, time floweth
coldly he blew his nose
reached a hand around his high round waist
            money was pinned to caftan
            aches & pains
a jew's a jew he says
love brings him to the words he needs
                    but sadly
        no
                    I cannot stay
                    for breakfast loving
                    the taste of duck eggs loving
                    little rolls & butter
                    loving cereals in metal pans
he tells them
                    all we touch is love
                    & feeds us
this is a portrait of a jew old country style
the gentile will fail to understand
the jew come on better days will run from it
how real
                    the grandfathers become
                    my grandfather the baker son of bakers
                    YOSEL DOVID ben SHMIEL
                    who was a hasid at the court in Rizhyn

came to U.S.A. circa 1913
but found the country godless
tho he worked in leather
shoes were the craft all our friends
got into first
e.g. his brother-in-law we called
THE UNCLE
I remember in a basement shop
somewhere "downtown"
bent over shoes he stitched
how many years would pass
till nineteen-fifty maybe
when I saw him last
his lungs gone in east bronx tenement
he slept behind a curtain
seeing me he thought
I was my brother   old & crazy
he was the oldest jew I knew
my grandfather had died
in nineteen-twenty
on the night my parents
ran to warsaw
to get married   my father
left for U.S.A. the next day
no one told him of his father's death
he would never be a talmudist
would go from shoes
to insurance
from insurance back to shoes
later an entrepreneur & bust
he was always clean

          shaven   my grandmother
          the religious one I mean
          saw the first beard
          I'd ever grown   got angry
          "jews don't wear beards"
          (she said) no
          not in golden U.S.A.
          the old man had fled from
          to his Polish death

for which reason I deny autobiography
or that the life of a man
matters more or less
          "We are all one man"
          Cezanne said
I count the failures of these jews
as proof of their election
they are divine because they all die

                              screaming
                    like the first

          universal jew
                    the gentiles
                         will tell you had some special deal

THE BROTHERS

to live with potatoes   not to eat them
but to live with them
they each had identical desires
& would surprise the neighbors by bellowing
if someone was good he was also
first & practical
wore long coats but kept the buttons
in his pockets   would paste
dollar bills in the pages of his books
while saying
                    the music that he heard
was "really" music   how are brothers
different? everyone would ask
the world would never recognize his beauty
found him "without love but blameless"
never certain who was walking beside him
he let his daughters dream about his sons
& vanished   it was nearly spring
but not in poland
brothers everywhere ran through the snow
spitting, my father said
they let the ice form on their hands
but more a question of politics
than of possessions   each man made his way
badly
grew up to lose a wad of cash
brothers with faces that were always old
they tried to sleep at odd hours
one masturbated to the age of fifty
smiling   one was always telling time
a loser's life

the brother sank deeper into his own business
at night the table danced   the house
had nearly come alive
& was dangerous
there was nothing to talk about so he listened
stunned by the taste of food
a fire in his jaw   here was his father
selling gloves again
one morning he saw a rooster in the elevator
could he think of names for it?
aladdin
abba
ahasuerus
every name he knew started with "a"
& pained him
now it pained him even more
he thought   the world
stopped being round or holding snow
women, slightly crazed
met him in the streets   daubed his hands
with goatshit
this was the key to paradise   the names
of paradise
were written in his heart
his brother told him
they were standing at a window crying
from their mouths
brothers have names to tell their shoes by
not their own   they were always old

THE MURDER INCORPORATED SUTRA

for Robert Kelly

Pincus Tavern
which Kelly passed
as schoolboy   den
of murderers or den of Jews
as murderers
no Benya Kriks he says
but bad guys simply
rotten
in the way America
disposes   though I pretend
other Pincus Taverns meetingplaces of one-eyed
hand in caftan hardcocked
Jewish bandits
beautiful men of noses enlarged with purple veins
of still-curled earlocks from childhood
who dared to cross the border in three coats
watchbands laid out from wrist to shoulders
but beardless could whistle
lost messages in secret Jewish code
meaning
"the Tsar's asshole smells of vinegar" etcetera
& were obliged to wield knives   not only
to cut a notch off a salami
but slit a windpipe
spreading his blood across
the merchant's vest or seeing
pictures in it
of rabbis with hardons unheard of
in the secular world
real to their perceptions who were
brothel Jews & inn-

keepers
expert in management of taverns
where most would let the Polacks
drink but took a piece
themselves if pressed to it
even would suck each other off
in Polish prisons
from there to Brooklyn emanations
made the journey   sought
Golden Kingdoms
at the corner of Stone & Sutter
(Kelly thought) some lounged
in doorways   improbable murderous Litvaks
with names like Lepke   Gurrah "Dutch Schultz"   Rothstein
        Lansky   Siegel
would drive wing'd cadillacs
with wraparound chrome exteriors of nineteen-thirty-one
to banquets on high holidays
eating turkey   chicken   goose with mushrooms
"a fish soup on which floated lakes of lemon juice"
drank velvety madeira booze from Canada cigars of J.P. Morgan
        sniffed cocaine sucked oranges
or dropped peels into their vodka
would wear a deluxe striped suit made of english navy
but with a head for business
Jews moved past el trains blasting tommy guns
other Jews made movies
ran after black girls   did a buck & wing
for Roman gangsters
toasted their mothers with hunky wines
that smelled of sun & bedbugs

of which the father of the dead man wrote in journal
"my child brings solace to a heavy heart
"his intense physicality
"not Jewish truly but tendering a dream of
"strength   resilience   broken promises
"a horsecock strapped between his legs
"in tribute   & my secret joy too
"seeing his dead frame surrounded
"by a thousand blossoms roses of old Poland
"a choir like the Warsaw Synagogue
"led by Sirota   bursts into songs of angels
"flashbulbs from fifty cameras pop
"blinding the humble button operators workers
"in black jackets & silk lapels some
"with yellow shoes   milk-stained wives   outclassed
"outdistanced by that stud in coffin
"whose hair pasted back still smells of
"whorehouse evenings along Atlantic Avenue
"not Moldavanka mad Odessa nights
"remembered the enforcers lift his coffin
"sweat stains the armpits of orange-colored suits
"strawberry vests   blue leather shoes
"& under the shirtcuff of the murdered son
"a diamond-studded bracelet"   thus
Babel or an uncle
might have written though the flesh
retreats from these as other
killers Jews who frightened the round-cheeked schoolboy
with gangster visions   of concrete
bodies into Catskill lakes
their fathers stood above & threw

lint from old pockets into
praying for joy   deliverance
from America the beautiful
oppressor riding in white convertible
up streets of Brownsville
the eagle of the golden States hooked on his arm
& hungry   diving
on faces that he hates
of Jew & Gentile
first searches their hearts for "freedom"
& the happy buck

THE STUDENT'S TESTIMONY

he was the last demon of ostrow
come back to visit & play
on my mind blowing delicious
bubbles of red soap into
the corners of the room
a furry singing little
demon with bulging eyes big
bulging balls & all
animal twisted into shapes
like rubber
"I love my demon" I would sing
& we would share the backroom of
the synagogue guzzling
the gentiles' beer &
snapping paperclips
against the rabbi's silks reliving
the poland of old friendships pork & fish
boiling & stinking in a single
pot we would dip our hands
into & make our bellies
shine
what grease
what aromas from the bookshelves
what smells of jews ripe for the sabbath
"fur" I would cry to him or "snot" & he
would wrap me in his sleeves & let
their velvet warm me
nightly the books were opening
in my dreams the letters
black as coal danced off
the page & fell on me I saw them

                    cross my hips & write the double
yod upon my cock
                              "never had Polish child felt
                    greater warmth beside her
mother than I felt there"
                              later the telephone came voices
                    reached us from "the kingdoms"
messages of love
                              vibrated there were calls
                    from warsaw krakow moscow kiev odessa
paris berlin new york london
                              buenos aires hongkong yokohama bombay
                    melbourne juneau tombstone perth
detroit johannesburg topeka east st louis
                              homesick we dreamed "freedom" meaning
                    that our hands could touch our feet reach
even the dirt between
                    the toes
                    & breathe its essence
(of a hundred slaughterhouses
                              the sweet fat of the sabbath
                    in our teeth we waited until the women
came to us bearing the bloody eyes
                    of cows & lambs
                    they piled up on the table crying
"hosanna to the gentiles")
                              buckwheat for dinner
                    in the lonely diner
eating globs of fat congealed
                              we played games near wealthy
                    homes pretending that we were children

"the luck of the jews"
                    "constantinople nights"
            "making the devil's mark on parchment"
also "the hair & beard of macroanthropos"
                    through which he led me his
            furry body hidden under
three suits of clothes towards other
                    pleasures secret holes
            he lived in
bathhouse partitions white with mold
                    & through a broken board the eye
            watched the old women strove to behold
the slit the fiery entranceway
                    dissolve
            the waters washing out the light the breath
that moves upon the waters
                    until the bulb above us splintered
            "god is one"
we sang my demon clung to me
                    made of my tongue
            his song
a master at pinochle sometimes
                    the deck flew in his hands
            beautiful men wept like children
some shelled almonds for him
                    or filled his hat with vodka
            the fat students loved him the dark ones
waited for news on the radio
                    "calm in the face of disaster"
            pilgrims visited the tsaddik's court he sat
for seven days

dipped figs in wine
then lifted his milkwhite hands each
finger held a garnet
each eye a golden tear
electricity ran from his beard he wore
a neon caftan
thrice did my demon limp into his presence
they were face to face neither
moving neither still in love
or heartsick
theirs was a meeting of the upper
& the lower worlds
the "model of the universe" was always
at their call an empty building windows
broken or taped-up with X's
in contrast to the tsaddik's its
easy warmth stoves in perfect order
so even a stranger had a place to sit
forgetful of each other
they let the time pass with singing not
with arithmetic
"a woman for me
& a woman for thee" (he would order)
the one with a wen near her nipple
the other with a glass eye women
with moist hair in their armpits
moister below
& furious
reputed to be in love with great men they were
"nieces" to all the rabbis
breathless my demon would mount his

                    from the rear the tsaddik
slept on in innocence of
                        heart & purpose
          barely
could feel her hand
                    betray him
          but blamed it on
the tightness of his linens while
                        wan allergic dreaming
          furry to his fingers
my demon
                    slept against the other's
          side forgetting
that the bride was always chaste the sabbath
                        always an interval
          between subscriptions
something cold but beautiful
                    not a mechanical process
          merely but responsive
to the touch
                    in satin slippers beneath
          a painted canopy
of stars each waited
                    for the bride
          each called her
sabbath but each had something else a different kind of sleep
                    in mind
. . . .

                              coda
                    once in a lifetime man
          may meet a hostile spirit once

he may be imprisoned for his
                    dreams & pay for them
            lightning is like oil the motor
once it starts keeps
                    running
            such was their wisdom though we had
no use for it
                    only later seeing it
            reborn
in joplin on a billboard
                    his own shadow
            was more than he could bear the war
came & he ran from it
                    back in the cellar drinking
            too much he grew thin
the great encounter ended it
                    in flames the candelabrum rose did it become
            a heart
that broke into sparks & letters
                    a shower of ruined cities from which
            my demon
vanished fled from the light when I was born

New Directions Paperbooks

Vladimir Nabokov, *Nikolai Gogol.* NDP78.
P. Neruda, *The Captain's Verses.*† NDP345.
  Residence on Earth.† NDP340.
New Directions 17. (Anthology) NDP103.
New Directions 18. (Anthology) NDP163.
New Directions 19. (Anthology) NDP214.
New Directions 20. (Anthology) NDP248.
New Directions 21. (Anthology) NDP277.
New Directions 22. (Anthology) NDP291.
New Directions 23. (Anthology) NDP315.
New Directions 24. (Anthology) NDP332.
New Directions 25. (Anthology) NDP339.
New Directions 26. (Anthology) NDP353.
New Directions 27. (Anthology) NDP359.
New Directions 28. (Anthology) NDP371.
New Directions 29. (Anthology) NDP378.
New Directions 30. (Anthology) NDP395.
Charles Olson, *Selected Writings.* NDP231.
George Oppen, *The Materials.* NDP122.
  Of Being Numerous. NDP245.
  This In Which. NDP201.
Wilfred Owen, *Collected Poems.* NDP210.
Nicanor Parra, *Emergency Poems.*† NDP333.
  Poems and Antipoems.† NDP242.
Boris Pasternak, *Safe Conduct.* NDP77.
Kenneth Patchen, *Aflame and Afun of*
    Walking Faces. NDP292.
  Because It Is. NDP83.
  But Even So. NDP265.
  Collected Poems. NDP284.
  Doubleheader. NDP211.
  Hallelujah Anyway. NDP219.
  In Quest of Candlelighters. NDP334.
  The Journal of Albion Moonlight. NDP99.
  Memoirs of a Shy Pornographer. NDP205.
  Selected Poems. NDP160.
  Sleepers Awake. NDP286.
  Wonderings. NDP320.
Octavio Paz, *Configurations.*† NDP303.
  Early Poems.† NDP354.
Plays for a New Theater. (Anth.) NDP216.
Ezra Pound, *ABC of Reading.* NDP89.
  Classic Noh Theatre of Japan. NDP79.
  The Confucian Odes. NDP81.
  Confucius. NDP285.
  Confucius to Cummings. (Anth.) NDP126.
  Gaudier-Brzeska. NDP372.
  Guide to Kulchur. NDP257.
  Literary Essays. NDP250.
  Love Poems of Ancient Egypt. NDP178.
  Pavannes and Divagations. NDP397.
  Pound/Joyce. NDP296.
  Selected Cantos. NDP304.
  Selected Letters 1907-1941. NDP317.
  Selected Poems. NDP66.
  Selected Prose 1909-1965. NDP396.
  The Spirit of Romance. NDP266.
  Translations.† (Enlarged Edition) NDP145.
Omar Pound, *Arabic and Persian Poems.*
  NDP305.
James Purdy, *Children Is All.* NDP327.
Raymond Queneau, *The Bark Tree.* NDP314.
  The Flight of Icarus. NDP358.
M. Randall, *Part of the Solution.* NDP350.
John Crowe Ransom, *Beating the Bushes.*
  NDP324.
Raja Rao, *Kanthapura.* NDP224.
Herbert Read, *The Green Child.* NDP208.
P. Reverdy, *Selected Poems.*† NDP346.
Kenneth Rexroth, *Assays.* NDP113.
  An Autobiographical Novel. NDP281.
  Beyond the Mountains. NDP384.
  Bird in the Bush. NDP80.
  Collected Longer Poems. NDP309.
  Collected Shorter Poems. NDP243.
  Love and the Turning Year. NDP308.
  New Poems. NDP383.

100 Poems from the Chinese. NDP192.
100 Poems from the Japanese.† NDP147.
Arthur Rimbaud, *Illuminations.*† NDP56.
  Season in Hell & Drunken Boat.† NDP97.
Selden Rodman, *Tongues of Fallen Angels.*
  NDP373.
Jerome Rothenberg, *Poland/1931.* NDP379.
Saikaku Ihara, *The Life of an Amorous*
    Woman. NDP270.
St. John of the Cross, *Poems.*† NDP341.
Jean-Paul Sartre, *Baudelaire.* NDP233.
  Nausea. NDP82.
  The Wall (Intimacy). NDP272.
Delmore Schwartz, *Selected Poems.* NDP241.
Stevie Smith, *Selected Poems.* NDP159.
Gary Snyder, *The Back Country.* NDP249.
  Earth House Hold. NDP267.
  Regarding Wave. NDP306.
  Turtle Island. NDP381.
Gilbert Sorrentino, *Splendide-Hôtel.* NDP364.
Enid Starkie, *Arthur Rimbaud.* NDP254.
Stendhal, *Lucien Leuwen.*
  Book II: *The Telegraph.* NDP108.
Jules Supervielle, *Selected Writings.*† NDP209.
W. Sutton, *American Free Verse.* NDP351.
Nathaniel Tarn, *Lyrics for the Bride of God.*
  NDP391.
Dylan Thomas, *Adventures in the Skin Trade.*
  NDP183.
  A Child's Christmas in Wales. NDP181.
  Collected Poems 1934-1952. NDP316.
  The Doctor and the Devils. NDP297.
  Portrait of the Artist as a Young Dog.
  NDP51.
  Quite Early One Morning. NDP90.
  Under Milk Wood. NDP73.
Lionel Trilling, *E. M. Forster.* NDP189.
Martin Turnell, *Art of French Fiction.* NDP251.
  Baudelaire. NDP336.
Paul Valéry, *Selected Writings.*† NDP184.
Elio Vittorini, *A Vittorini Omnibus.* NDP366.
  Women of Messina. NDP365.
Vernon Watkins, *Selected Poems.* NDP221.
Nathanael West, *Miss Lonelyhearts &*
  Day of the Locust. NDP125.
George F. Whicher, tr.,
  The Goliard Poets.† NDP206.
J. Willett, *Theatre of Bertolt Brecht.* NDP244.
J. Williams, *An Ear in Bartram's Tree.* NDP335.
Tennessee Williams, *Camino Real.* NDP301.
  Cat on a Hot Tin Roof. NDP398.
  Dragon Country. NDP287.
  Eight Mortal Ladies Possessed. NDP374.
  The Glass Menagerie. NDP218.
  Hard Candy. NDP225.
  In the Winter of Cities. NDP154.
  One Arm & Other Stories. NDP237.
  Out Cry. NDP367.
  The Roman Spring of Mrs. Stone. NDP271.
  Small Craft Warnings. NDP348.
  27 Wagons Full of Cotton. NDP217.
William Carlos Williams,
  The Autobiography. NDP223.
  The Build-up. NDP259.
  The Farmers' Daughters. NDP106.
  Imaginations. NDP329.
  In the American Grain. NDP53.
  In the Money. NDP240.
  Many Loves. NDP191.
  Paterson. Complete. NDP152.
  Pictures from Brueghel. NDP118.
  The Selected Essays. NDP273.
  Selected Poems. NDP131.
  A Voyage to Pagany. NDP307.
  White Mule. NDP226.
  W. C. Williams Reader. NDP282.
Yvor Winters,
  Edwin Arlington Robinson. NDP326.

Complete descriptive catalog available free on request from
New Directions, 333 Sixth Avenue, New York 10014.   † Bilingual